The Dance in Theory

THE ——— DANCE —— IN THEORY

by John Martin

With a New Introduction
by Jack Anderson

A Dance Horizons Book
Princeton Book Company, Publishers
Princeton, NJ

The Dance in Theory is a reprint of pages 31–126 of
Introduction to the Dance, originally published in 1939
by W. W. Norton & Co., Inc., New York

A Dance Horizons Book
Princeton Book Company, Publishers
POB 57
Pennington, NJ 08534

Library of Congress Cataloging-in-Publication Data

Martin, John Joseph, 1893-
    The dance in theory.

    "A Dance Horizons book."
    "Reprint of pages 31-126 of Introduction to the dance,
originally published in 1939 by W.W. Norton & Co., Inc.,
New York"--T.p. verso.
    1. Modern dance--United States--History. I. Title.
GV1783.M328 1989   792.8'0973   89-24192
ISBN 0-916622-90-8

Contents

INTRODUCTION

❧❧❧❧❧❧

THE thoughtfulness of his writing would have made John Martin a major dance critic at any time. But several factors also helped make him especially important at a particular period in the development of American dance and dance journalism. Long after his retirement in 1962 and his death in 1985, he remains one of our most provocative critics.

He arrived on the scene early, publishing his first review in the *New York Times* in 1927. That year, Helen Tamiris rejected her Metropolitan Opera Ballet training and resolved to become a modern dancer. The year before, Martha Graham had made her New York debut. In 1928, Doris Humphrey and Charles Weidman would form their own new company. As far as serious American dance—particularly American modern dance—was concerned, Martin was present almost at the creation, and he was from the very start of his critical career a firm supporter of the modern dancers.

Yet he cannot be called our first American dance critic. Earlier in the century, and also in the *Times*, Carl van Vechten had written sensitively about dance. H. T. Parker reviewed dance in the *Boston Evening Transcript* from 1905 to 1934. And only a few weeks before Martin came to the *Times*, Mary F.

Watkins was appointed dance critic of the *Herald Tribune*. However, van Vechten and Parker were music critics who covered dance as an adjunct to their music-reviewing assignments. Watkins had also been a music critic before she turned to dance, and her tenure as a dance critic lasted only until 1934.

Martin stayed on until 1962—and he stayed on at the *Times*. New York has been the home of many newspapers, good and bad. But no paper (with the possible exception of the now-defunct *Herald Tribune*) has gained a reputation like that of the *Times*. Because the *Times* sought to keep up with the arts, it was eagerly scanned by actors, playwrights, musicians, and impresarios. It still remains a matter for debate whether a *Times* review can, or ever could, literally make or break a show. Nevertheless, a *Times* review has always "meant something." The fact that the *Times* was willing to hire a dance reviewer therefore meant that dance was obviously worth taking seriously. And Martin—with his grave, even slightly schoolmasterish, prose—was very serious indeed.

Martin's interest in dance developed out of his interest in the other arts. He was born in Louisville, Kentucky, in 1893; his father was a purchasing agent with the Louisville and Nashville Railway and his mother was a singer. He attended the University of Louisville, majoring in classics, then went to Chicago to study violin at the Chicago Conservatory. In Chicago, he became involved with one of the pioneering community theatre groups of the time, the Chicago Little Theatre. It was also in Chicago that he met Hettie Louise Mick, an actress and puppeteer who was his wife from 1918 until her death in 1954. During World War I, he served with the U.S. Army Air Force Signal Corps.

Moving to New York, Martin served as an editor of the *Dramatic Mirror*, a trade publication, from 1919 to 1922. In 1922 he also began working in a press agent's office, while from 1924 to 1926 he was the executive director of Richard Boleslavsky's Laboratory Theatre. He applied for a reviewing post at the *Times* when a mutual friend told him that Olin Downes, of the paper's music staff, felt overworked having to cover both music and dance. Yet, even after he began writing for the *Times*, Martin did not totally abandon the theatre. Because there was no summer dance season in New York in those days, the summer months left him free to direct plays, which he did for summer-stock companies in Johnstown, Pennsylvania (1929), Locust Valley, New York (1933), and New Rochelle, New York (1934).

Martin impressed many people as an austere man. Although he could relax and be sociable with close friends, casual acquaintances sometimes found him almost forbiddingly dignified. Unlike Walter Terry in his later years, Martin as he grew older did not often encourage young dance writers. And even after he left the *Times* he still remained aloof, in contrast to Edwin Denby, who seemed to enjoy playing the role of elder statesman and who could often be seen in theatre lobbies chatting with dancers, poets, and artists. Martin kept his distance. Significantly, a 1958 biography of him in *Times Talk*, a publication for and about *Times* employees, was titled "Inscrutable Dance Man." Yet he was not totally reclusive for, after he left the *Times*, he taught at the University of California at Los Angeles and in summers at the American Dance Festival at Connecticut College, just as during the 1930s he had taught at the Bennington College summer sessions.

Some observers have charged that Martin soured slightly as a critic over the years. But he had always been controversial. Many ballet fans reacted violently to his early criticism of Balanchine. And some modern dance lovers lamented that Martin appeared to have little sympathy for newer developments in the very art he had once championed.

But both his encomiums and his diatribes arose out of something more than whim. Martin had theories about dance and, what's more, he was willing to argue them in print. Presumably, all critics have theories of some sort; one cannot be involved in an art for any length of time without developing some ideas, however hazy, of that art's nature and of the way it works. But critics do not always express these ideas at length. Nor do they have to, for critics—especially, given the nature of their jobs, newspaper critics—are more often called upon to analyze specific works of art than to propound general theories. The theory from which their analyses derive may, of course, be implicit in their writing, but the formulation or defense of that theory will not ordinarily be the point of the review.

It is also risky to state generalized theories in print, for aesthetic theories have a nasty habit of proving inadequate. Just about any theory can be attacked, if its opponent is only diligent and clever enough. And, at times, art may change so unpredictably that theorists may feel obliged either to modify their ideas in order to account for the art or to denounce the art in order to cling to their ideas. If art were not protean and theories were not vulnerable, aesthetics and criticism might have stopped with Aristotle.

John Martin took risks; he not only developed theories about dance, he stated them clearly. Fortunately, they were not foolish. When examined today, they reveal that Martin thoroughly understood what the early modern dancers were up to. It is no wonder, then, that he became a persuasive spokesman for them. At least two formulations of his theories remain of interest. Martin's basic ideas are lucidly stated in *The Modern Dance* (originally published by A. S. Barnes & Co. in 1933 and reprinted by Dance Horizons). He developed them further in his *Introduction to the Dance*—the book puɒ-lished by W. W. Norton & Co. in 1939 from which the excerpts reprinted here derive.

Many of Martin's basic theories have not lost their validity, although some may have to be reformulated slightly to make them applicable to the dance of a later time. Moreover, reading them a half-century after Martin first formulated them may make one realize that theories are not necessarily only the result of pure disinterested reasoning: the most loftily Olympian of theories may also be ways of advancing a critic's personal enthusiasms or prejudices.

As he wrote in his *Introduction to the Dance*, Martin believed that "Good art speaks directly from its creator's emotions to our own." Of all arts, dance may be the one that is closest to life experience, for it involves the human body moving in reaction to its environment. For Martin, there are at least three types of dance: recreational, spectacular, and expressional. Recreational dance is dance performed primarily for the edification or amusement of the participants. Such dance can be lofty (as ceremonial dances are) or merely entertaining (as most ballroom dances are), but they do not necessarily require spectators. However, both spectacular and expressional dance are theatrical forms: Their creators assume there will be an audience watching them.

In spectacular dance, the emphasis is not upon what the movement "says" to the spectator, but upon what it looks like. In expressional dance, the emphasis is entirely upon what the movement "says." The types of spectacular dance that Martin lists in the second section of *Introduction to the Dance* include tap, acrobatic adagio, "fan" and "bubble" dancing, and ballet. However, about the only type of dance that fully qualifies as expressional is modern dance. Martin wonders what ancient

Greek dance might have been like, but because examples of it have not survived, he wisely refrains from making sweeping generalizations about it.

Martin's categorizations are intellectually provocative; they are also symptomatic of his own personal taste. Martin, the tireless supporter of modern dance, finds that art to be the only extant dance form that is truly expressional; and, though he professes to respect ballet, he nevertheless places it in a category along with types of dance that some viewers might consider escapist or downright trivial.

Whatever one may think of his categories, one can only applaud Martin for proceeding to raise one of the great questions of dance theory: How does dance movement communicate? It could be argued that no one has ever come up with a totally convincing answer to that question. But Martin's answer is at least worth considering.

Martin believes that dance movement communicates to an audience by a process of kinetic transfer he calls metakinesis. In his *Introductions to the Dance* he states that dancers organize the movements in their works to produce specific reactions in their audience. The movements serve as kinetic stimuli and viewers respond to them with muscular sympathy. These responses need not be, and often are not, overt; instead, the response may be entirely a matter of inner mimicry.

The belief that all movements convey some sort of meaning was held by many of the actors of Martin's time who were influenced by the acting theories of Konstantin Stanislavsky and the productions of the Moscow Art Theatre. As a former actor and director, Martin would have been well aware of them. Since motivated movement was also one of the concerns of the early modern dancers, it is not surprising that Martin responded sympathetically to their endeavors.

The fact that dances could be kinetic revelations encouraged experimentation, since traditional forms could easily prove inadequate to convey fresh revelations. "Form is not a separate entity," said Martin in his *Introduction to the Dance*, "and cannot exist apart from materials ... the purpose of form is the shaping of material so that it fulfills a specific function...."

Because he sought to demonstrate that dance was a serious art, Martin distrusted frivolity. But this severity of taste led to a distrust of sensual appeals that may now strike us as unduly puritanical. In part, Martin's severity may have arisen from a desire to prevent a "spectacular" art like ballet from blinding audiences to the merits of the "expressional" art of modern dance. Yet some of his views do seem extreme. Design, he wrote in *The Modern Dance*, "can never ... be productive of anything even at its best beyond pleasure to the eye." To anyone who might wonder, "What's wrong with that?" he warned in the same volume, "The senses are channels by means of which contact is established with the outside world. The beauty which serves to fill them only impedes this contact."

To carry the extremist aspects of Martin's theories even further, one could argue that since modern dance offers revelations and design can be sensually distracting, then the highest form of modern dance must be the solo, since the presence of at least one other dancer on stage might introduce distracting elements of design into the composition. Martin himself went to that extreme in an essay in the *Dance Encyclopedia* (edited by Anatole Chujoy and P. W. Manchester and published in 1967), saying, "In its essence the new dance was the externalization of a single individual's intensely personal vision. As such it was necessarily a solo art. When it sought to widen its scope by the inclusion of other dancers it embarked unwittingly on the route of self-destruction...." Martin had not always been so narrow in his attitudes: during the 30's he had identified modern dance's greatest triumphs as the choreography of Mary Wigman (who created both solos and group works) and Doris Humphrey's *New Dance* trilogy (one of the most ambitious ensemble compositions in all modern dance).

By the 1960's, he believed that the original creative impulses of modern dance had been diluted or corrupted by increasing theatricalization and by a preoccupation with form for its own sake. Theatricalization meant that a dance was no longer a personal vision; now, it could be a great stage picture (or series of constantly changing pictures). Unabashedly theatrical dances—and Martin specifically praises Martha Graham's *Clytemnestra* as one of them—could be profound or tragic. Yet they differed somewhat in nature from the early expressional modern dances.

The way some newer modern dance choreographers moved from a concern for motivation to a preoccupation with design, structure, form, and—among the real mavericks—anti-form annoyed Martin, for such a development seemed a rejection of the achievements of those choreographers' illustrious elders. So, in *The Dance Encyclopedia*, Martin laments that "decadent influences ruled out as old-fashioned and bourgeois the concept of inner vision as the invoker of art and substituted chance and happenstance; adding palindromes, interchangeable phrases, and esoteric and contrived mathematical formulas as methods of composition ... this self-styled avant-garde proved only to have led itself into a blind alley in which to play what amounted to cynical games of jackstones with the bones of the prophets."

In reply, it could be said that Martin himself may have been led if not into a blind alley, then at least into a tight corner by a combination of personal taste (he did not like some of the specific dances he was seeing) and intellectual theory (his ideas about how modern dance works, or ought to work, did little to explicate or justify these dances). Many observers today may feel that Martin treated his categories of dance as if they were rigid, rather than merely suggestive, distinctions. After all, Martin's own theories of the power of movement mean that even the most spectacular of dances must be somehow, if only slightly, expressive; and given the fact that they are necessarily performed by three-dimensional moving bodies, even the most determinedly expressional dances must have some sort of visual appeal on stage.

However, if Martin's categories are unnecessarily limiting, his concept of kinetic transfer may still be valid. Indeed, that concept may help us understand the appeal of many disparate dance forms. In his *Introduction to the Dance*, Martin specifically says that "No movement of the human body is possible without definite relation to life experience, even if it is random or inadvertent." He also says that "in any movement or posture, however based merely on laws of design, there is bound to be an implication either of motivation or else of the inco-ordinations of mental unbalance."

This means, among other things, that any movement a choreographer thinks appropriate—however rough or polished, pedestrian or virtuosic—may legitimately function as a dance movement and that many types—on occasion, even unfamiliar types—of dance may communicate to us. Kinetic transfer may help explain why dances arising out of the history and customs of distant continents may occasionally touch us deeply and why our feelings may be stirred by abstract ballets. The experience of seeing carefully patterned choreographic designs may be one of beholding images of order or harmony, and the dissolution of such patterns may have the effect of an emotional rendering. Even the constantly changing currents of "chance" dances may invigorate or disquiet us because we sense in them some of the same currents of life as it is lived outside the theatre in the streets.

Believing that Martin's general theories of metakinesis retain at least a measure of validity does not mean that one is committed to like only the kinds of choreography he did. Martin's concept is more inclusive than his taste. It is perhaps worth noting that Charles Olson, the poet whose idea of literary transfer parallels Martin's idea of kinetic transfer, participated in a mixed-media event at Black Mountain College in 1952 that is often regarded as the first "happening." Other participants included the choreographer Merce Cunningham and the composer John Cage, two of the experimenters to whom Martin may have been alluding in his unfavorable remarks in *The Dance Encyclopedia*.

Whatever his quirks of taste may have been, it now appears that Martin was remarkably prophetic on occasion. Writing in the *New York Times* on 27 November 1927, he said, "The amazing growth of the art consciousness of the American people during the last 20 years is nowhere more clearly manifested than in the field of the dance." Looking back, it might seem that in 1927 American dance was only in its infancy. Martin's assertion sounds like sheer bravado. Yet Martin knew how to analyze the dance he saw about him and he could foresee what it was capable of developing into.

His views and the way he phrased them reflect some of the aesthetic attitudes that flourished during a certain period in the development of modern theatre and modern dance. Yet his essential vision of dance is capable of transcending the particular period in which he wrote his criticism. John Martin still provides us with much to think about.

Jack Anderson

Chapter One

THE NATURE OF MOVEMENT

I N spite of the fact that the dance is perhaps the least generally understood of all the arts, it employs as its medium a material that is closer to life experience than that employed by any of the other arts, namely, the movement of the body in its reactions to its environment. This, indeed, is the very stuff of life. Instead of contributing to the easy understanding of the dance, however, this fact has actually worked in the opposite direction. The movement of the body is so habitual, so continuous, and so largely automatic that we are in the main quite unconscious of its range and potentialities. Familiarity breeds not contempt, perhaps, but certainly neglect. We are most likely to forget altogether that, besides its more obvious functions of locomotion and the like, movement is a vigorous medium for both expression and perception. If we are to have any practical concept of the dance, however, we must become keenly aware of it in both these capacities, for not only does the dancer employ movement to express his ideas, but, strange as it may seem, the spectator must also employ movement in order to respond to the dancer's intention and understand what he is trying to convey.

It is imperative here, accordingly, that we postpone all concentration on the dance itself until we shall have familiarized ourselves with the processes that underlie it. This will take us necessarily into a consideration of the psychological factors that make movement a means of perception, of its functions in the practical and the imaginative life, and of the part it plays in all art experience. It is not until we have isolated the substance of which dance is made, as we shall do in this chapter, and have seen the process of composition by which it is put into intelligible form, as we shall do in the next chapter, that the dance can begin to emerge whole.

In everyday life our first reaction to every object and circumstance is in terms of movement, for, as we shall see presently, that is the way living creatures are constituted for their protection and survival. It is natural, therefore, that the earliest art impulses to make their appearance in human history use this most elementary of all mediums as their material. As a matter of fact, even most of the lower animals, including birds and fish, are known to dance.

When primitive man wants to experience something that his immediate environment does not provide for him, he creates an imaginary environment in which he can realize these needs, at least temporarily. Since his capacity for life experience at the moment exceeds his opportunity for living, he must provide himself with a synthetic outlet as much like life experience as possible. To this imaginary environment that he creates for the purpose, he responds just as if it were actual; that is, he reacts first in terms of movement, or in other words, he dances. His activity is perhaps play rather than art at this level, since it may lack altogether the element of communication, but of that more later. For the present, let it suffice that the medium in which the art impulse first expresses itself is that of movement. No matter how many later developments it may undergo which may refine the element of overt movement to the vanishing point, no matter how sophisticated, how abstract, how involved it may become, movement is still its root.

The spectator's approach brings another angle to bear on the essential facts of movement. All too frequently the spectator is believed to have nothing to do except to bring himself into the general vicinity of a symphony, a painting, a dance, and let something mysterious called beauty or art pour itself over him as sunlight pours itself over a table that chances to be in its path. But if a man made no more active response to art than the table to sunlight he would experience no more reaction. On the other hand, there are many conscientious followers of the arts who go to the opposite extreme. Realizing that they must play some more active part than this in their contact with art, they accordingly concentrate all their intellectual powers on analyzing its make-up, figuring out its technical details, and trying to deduce its probable meaning from these data. It would be hard to say which approach is the more futile and unrewarding.

It is virtually a truism that nothing is ever understood until it is translated into terms of experience. We may accept something in theory if it comes to us on reliable authority, but it is not actually ours until we have put it into action, whether it happens to be a cooking receipt, an engineering formula, a route of travel, a landscape, or a work of art. The question, then, is how do we put a work of art into action so that it becomes ours? Let us resort to a crude analogy.

When a Christmas pudding is set before us, we go at it with delight, knowing from previous association with Christmas puddings what an agreeable experience it is. But the pudding means nothing at all to us until we taste it, and even then there is only a momentary gustatory pleasure which contains no satisfaction. On the contrary, it merely whets the appetite, and the adventure is not complete until we have actually eaten the pudding. We have really enjoyed the experience and profited by it only when the pudding has gone through the processes of deglutition and digestion and its nutritious elements have been absorbed into the system to build up blood, bone, muscle. In other words, the total experience of pudding involves the breaking down of the whole into its essential components and the distribution of these where they will be efficacious. We cannot simply subject ourselves to a Christmas pudding, nor is there any known means by which it can automatically inject itself into the system in toto as an entity; it must first be changed into a more assimilable form. The greater part of this transformation is, of course, automatic; once we have chewed and swallowed the delightful morsel, our volitional part of the activity is over.

The enjoyment of a work of art is in the main a parallel process. It is possible to stop at the stage of merely "tasting" it—that is, admiring its color, shape, rhythm—but that is an unsatisfying and profitless method of procedure, in spite of its prevalence. The actual digestion of a work of art demands no more deliberate activity than that of a pudding, but it must be "chewed" and "swallowed" so that it can be brought into contact with the necessary mechanism. The rest is done without effort of will, but it is done, nevertheless, by dynamic processes. We have no experience of art until it has been transmuted into assimilable stuff, and this assimilable stuff is the stuff of life experience, which in its basic terms is movement.

In our reception of a work of art, it is those elements in it which awaken experiences out of our own background that give it value for us, for nothing outside experience can possibly have meaning. Art is not, however, merely a means for reliving the past; its only relation to the past is to give it focus, drawing out of the haphazard miscellany which constitutes one's background a clearly defined body of experiences, seen now for the first time under the artist's stimulus, as belonging not to an isolated period gone by but as giving meaning to the present. Thus in the instant of revelation, past and present illumine each other, and the process itself adds a still further immediate experience, a quickening synthesis which actual life environment at the moment could not provide alone.

The artist, who in all likelihood does not even know of our personal existence, much less of our particular backgrounds, has built in terms of universal experience as he has touched it in his own life, and in proportion to the breadth of contacts with universal experience which each of us has stored up, his work is capable of awakening us to a moment of richer and fuller living. There is a widespread sentimental attitude toward art which assumes that its sole function is the bringing up of images of roses, babies' smiles, and other fortuitous fantasies, but actually its evocations are not of promiscuous and random images of any sort. The artist's efforts are directed toward touching into life specific experiences definitely related to the material he has selected, and his arrangement of it is all to this end. Though the entire activity takes place below the intellectual level, it is not for this reason vague or indeterminate, nor are its results extraneous to its substance and content.

For some of us certain components of any work of art will probably produce keener reactions than others, so that not all of us will react alike. In the eating of the pudding, one man may merely have endured the raisins, another have wished that the citron had been omitted, a third may have had a cold in the head and tasted the whole pudding less sharply, and a fourth may have found it too rich and too heavy and passed it by altogether. Our total reactions, whether to pudding or work of art, depend upon the equipment we bring to bear upon it, our past experience and present expectation.

We may like or dislike a work of art as we may a pudding, and this decision is not necessarily either arbitrary or whimsical but functional. When we are left unmoved it is either because our background does not contain associations of the nature demanded, or what is far more likely, because our apparatus for aesthetic digestion is unable to cope with the situation. Obviously all cases of aesthetic indigestion come from inability to break down works of art into assimilable material, that is, into terms of life experience, which is only another way of saying movement.

Work, Play and Art

It may be a totally unfamiliar idea to many people to have life experience made synonymous with movement in this way, for movement is taken pretty thoroughly for granted. It is easy to overlook the fact that it constitutes the chief substance of daily living and thinking. The common habit is to divide experience into two departments, action and thought, and to consider the latter somehow on a higher plane. When the subject is examined a little more closely, however, thinking itself is seen to be dynamic; no matter how deeply introspective it may be, it must go back ultimately to some concrete experience with the outside world, which is to say, some experience of movement. Otherwise it would have to exist virtually in a vacuum, and having nothing to deal with, could not actually exist at all.

Like thinking, art cannot exist in a vacuum, but must have constant reference to life, and this, obviously, through the ordinary functions of movement. It is well, then, to consider in a brief and general way what the ordinary functions of movement are in daily life, and their possibilities for translation into art.

In the illustration of the pudding, its essential value was found to consist in its contribution to the "inner man," and this provides a fitting point of attack upon the problem. It has become a kind of standard joke to refer to eating as appeasing the "inner man," and like many other jokes, it comes nearer to the truth than we are likely to realize. No doubt the reference is habitually turned into playfulness because of our inheritance from the Victorian age of the notion that the body and all its organic functionings are gross and inferior while the higher nature consists entirely of cerebration and fantasy. It would consequently be a trifle grotesque with such an upbringing to admit that the "inner man," the nucleus of the personality, is primarily concerned with eating and drinking and other equally low and vulgar matters. Nevertheless, if we are willing to put aside pretty poetic concepts, in the interest of something nearer to biological truth, we shall see that cerebration and fantasy and all the many ramifications of the so-called higher mental life have been evolved and exist solely for the service of the somewhat crude "inner man" about which we jest so lightly.

The actual inner man, which dominates the personality with its demands, consists of those elements of the organism which serve to maintain life and keep it functioning at a harmonious level. They are made up in general of what are sometimes called the vital organs, along with a virtually independent nervous system of their own. Here, with due apologies to our Victorian forebears for the indelicacy of the idea, is where our emotional life is born, rather than in any ethereal departments of the mind, for our emotions are nothing more than stirred-up states resulting from the action of these prosaic organs when they are confronted with objects or situations which have bearing upon their well-being, either to menace or to augment it. Manifestly a stirred-up state is not a state in which life can function at a harmonious level, and must be alleviated before the inner man can proceed at his normal pace. In the alleviation of these states most of our life experience and all of our art is brought into being. In an uninterrupted and self-perpetuating vegetative state there would be no demands, no upheavals, no art, and no growth.

Nature, however, has apparently decreed that there shall be no such static condition. The inner man must get food from his environment and must be protected from anything in that environment that might tend to injure or destroy him. The very fact that obviously he must exist in an environment of some sort, provides the necessity for all sorts of contacts—with objects that are desirable to acquire, with those that must be fled from, and with those that must be destroyed. Indeed, not maintenance of life alone constitutes nature's minimum requirement, but growth as well, for the one cannot exist without the other.

But not being able to live in his own self-contained universe puts the inner man into something of a predicament. Consisting as he does of a few organs with definitely limited functions, he would be doomed to practically immediate annihilation if he did not have some outside assistance. He has no means whatever for providing himself with food, and if something should come along and threaten to trample him underfoot he is without any way of removing himself from the zone of danger. Tucked neatly away somewhere in the middle of the body, he has no powers of locomotion and no direct contact with the outside world. He can only make his wants known—and this he can do with some vigor—and leave it to some other agency to fulfill them.

This outward body that he is tucked inside of comprises the agency that nature has evolved for him for this purpose, and a remarkably delicate and dexterous agency it is in its entirety. It contains a number of bony levers and an intricate structure of active muscles to operate them so as to make it possible to move toward objects or away from them, to acquire them or destroy them; countless sense organs placed strategically so as to serve as channels for becoming aware of these objects in the outside world and for reporting their character; and a complex system of nerves and brain cells to co-ordinate the senses' reports on such objects with the inner man's estimate of them, and to make the necessary connections for appropriate action of muscles, arms and legs, etc., toward them. The inner man alone determines what he needs and desires and must have; it is up to the outer man to locate these necessities, figure out how to secure them, and bring them into the sphere of the inner man's activity.

This problem involves a number of different kinds of action, since the necessities of the inner man are many and varied. Action, of course, means movement; and movement in general, therefore, divides itself automatically into several major classifications according to the exigencies of the situation.

There are, first of all, those movements which supply the bare essentials of life, with the emotional nature left as much out of consideration as it is possible to leave it in theory. These are grouped together in the category of work, and include the getting of food, the chopping of wood and drawing of water, the maintaining of cleanliness, protection from the elements—in short, all the routine of sustaining life on the most harmonious level with the smallest expenditure of energy. A great many of these movements are instinctive, while a great many others are the result of learning and are actually highly specialized skills.

It is possible theoretically to conceive of an environment in which the needs of the inner man are so nicely balanced with the ability of the outer man to supply them that no other forms of activity are necessary to maintain the organism in perfect trim. This is an environment, however, that is entirely nonexistent, for in any actual life situation there occur conditions which tend to overtax the ability of the outer man, and which consequently increase the demands of the inner man beyond the point where an even balance of harmonious functioning is possible. In a complex world where there are conflicts and repressions on every hand, the demands of the emotional life become far greater than can be easily satisfied in the actual life situation. It is necessary, then, for the ingenious outer man from time to time to create a fictitious, a synthetic, an ideal life situation in which satisfaction is possible.

Play and art are the chief divisions of this creative life. They are closely related to each other, and obviously cannot depart entirely from the character of work movements, since these are the only movements that come naturally into experience. They are, however, an extension and adaptation of work movements beyond their normal limitations, or else they would serve no end that work itself might not serve.

Play, whether it takes the form of daydreaming or of strenuous physical exercise, is essentially an ingoing activity, so to speak. In it the child (or the man, for that matter) employs skills which his life situation tends to stultify, or extends them beyond the point where they have been proved safe in practical life. If a second person is involved, it is only to intensify the player's reaction. For example, it gives a keener pleasure to dance in unison with others than to dance alone, in that each dancer is thus able to participate in a total movement experience greater in strength and scope than any of them could create alone. There is, however, no exchange of emotional concepts, nothing created. The relationship between them is one of mutual awareness rather than of communication.

Art, on the other hand, is an outgoing activity. It demands response or the expectation of response. The poet, the musician, the painter, the actor, or the dancer, does not create his work for the mere pleasure of the process but always with the vision that the work itself, once created, will give back to those who see or hear it something of what he has put into it. From this vision he derives his satisfaction. He makes art only because he conceives of truths which cannot be realized in his current daily experience but which must nevertheless be realized and recognized as truths if only in a synthetic world. Since he has conceived them he must externalize them. These truths inevitably involve not the artist alone but a sense of the potentialities that exist in the relationship between men or between man and his environment, and hence cannot be objectified in solitude. He is perhaps asking for co-operation in the attainment of a fuller and richer life which he has glimpsed and cannot attain without the aid of his fellows. At the least he is recording a revelation which he himself may return to and re-enjoy in the capacity of spectator.

The ultimate distinction, then, between play and art is this matter of communication, which the former lacks and the latter demands. Whatever the specific forms of either may be, however, they must be referred back ultimately to the inner man for approval, no matter how successful they may seem to the reason and ingenuity of the outer man who has made them. He does not feel, he only thinks and devises.

By our sterner ancestors both play and art were frowned upon as impractical, wasteful, a flight into unreality, and hence immoral, and the same viewpoint prevails among ascetics of various types today. That it is an untenable position to take, however, needs hardly to be argued. In play, aside from its immediate satisfactions, the child learns skills and adaptations, both physical and emotional, which develop enormously his capacity for meeting the problems of practical life. Its values have become so widely recognized that it now finds a place in the formal educational program in all enlightened communities. Similarly, art provides an extension of the emotional potentialities, leading to easier adjustments, larger tolerances, broader visions. When vague and half-felt needs are brought to light and synthetically satisfied for a moment in the imaginative world of art, the first step has been taken on the road to their more realistic satisfaction in life. Thus, though the senses, nerves and muscles have no traffic whatever with morality, their ultimate action in both play and art is to increase the powers and extend the range of all men's lives.

Movement Sense

SINCE the efforts of the outer man to carry out his orders from within constitute the sum total of what we are aware of as the business of living, whether in work, play or art, it is well to consider briefly not only the motivations of such efforts, but also what they consist of fundamentally and how they operate.

As has already been pointed out, our only possible contact with the outside world is through the senses. When a sense impression is made upon any of the countless receptors provided for the purpose in the eyes, ears, skin, etc., it is borne at once through the nerves to the spinal cord and brain, where, as in an elaborate telephone exchange, it is instantly transformed into an outgoing impulse over other nerves to certain appropriate muscles and glands to prepare them for movement. When it is recalled that the entire sense mechanism has evolved purely to establish contact with outside objects so that they can be adapted to the use of the organism, it will be readily seen that the only function of sense impressions is to prepare the body for appropriate movement with relation to the objects reported upon. It follows, then, that we are made aware of any object only in terms of the appropriate movement we are prepared to make with relation to it.

It is not necessary, to be sure, for the body to make all the movements for which it is prepared by the reports of the senses; past experience has shown, for example, that many noises that strike the ear are not indicative of dangers that must be fled from, and the actual carrying out of the movement for which the muscles are prepared is inhibited by this knowledge. The impulse is, so to speak, short-circuited. Also, many circuits of sense impression and movement have become so familiar with repetition that they have made well-worn paths for themselves in the neuromuscular system and now operate without our even being aware of them. A circuit that is often traversed becomes, as in any other travel route, increasingly familiar with each repetition until it is virtually automatic.

Manifestly the number of sense impressions and their corresponding motor preparations in a day is tremendous, for we are constantly seeing, hearing, touching, smelling, and tasting things. But the sum total of all these sensorimotor experiences is still less than those which come from another source, a source which is commonly ignored altogether. However little we are aware of it, we are fortunately equipped with a sixth sense which concerns not so much the outside world directly as that elaborate and intricate world which is comprised in the body itself. This is a movement sense. Sense organs are to be found in the tissue of the muscles and in the joints, which respond to movements of the body in much the same way that the eye responds to light or the ear to sound. They register change of posture however small throughout the body, and thus tend to keep it always in alignment, so to speak.

When a traveler picks up his suitcase its weight would probably pull him off his feet if it were not that he has sense receptors which report the movement he has made and give a signal, as it were, to set up an equal pull elsewhere in the body to offset the strain. A moment later he is stepping with one foot upon a high coach step and would again be in a precarious condition if his body were not given sufficient information to establish the proper compensations. Consider, also, the predicament of the pianist if, literally as well as figuratively speaking, his left hand did not know what his right hand were doing. Or what might happen to the baseball pitcher when he winds up if his body were not kept constantly informed of his movements so as to make the necessary adjustments? Or what of the dancer poised *en arabesque* on the tip of one toe? Or the oarsman if he could not pull equally on both sides? Or the surgeon if he had no way of sensing the gradations of movement involved in a delicate operation?

These movement-sense receptors comprise certainly the busiest system in the entire body, for we are in a continual state of postural change, far greater than we realize, from the movement of the eyeballs in following an object, to the periodic contractions of the stomach. Besides the receptors in the muscle tissue, there are also semicircular canals in the ears which collaborate in recording data concerning our balance and tendencies to shift from it. If we did not have this testimony, we should be perpetually falling down, or even unaware of whether we were right side up or upside down. Through the agency of movement sense we are able to regulate the force of our movements, to co-ordinate them so that objects can be picked up or put down, and to make hundreds more otherwise impossible motor adjustments without which we could not begin to carry on a single day's normal activity.

Just as we found some paths well worn in that part of the sensorimotor system which deals with reports of the outside world, so we find similar beaten tracks in this inner system. These well-established patterns provide us with a great deal of background information and save us incalculable effort and experimentation. To take a simple example: when we consider the weight of a log that we chance to see lying across the path, there is awakened in us a pattern of movement responses based on memory of previous experiences with the weight of objects which prepares us through our movement sense for the muscular forces that will be brought into play and the energy involved in lifting this particular log. We need not actually lift it, therefore, to know that it is heavy, and approximately how heavy. The report made by the eye is sufficient to open one of many beaten tracks in our neuromuscular experience and associate this object with previous objects with which we have had contact. When we pronounce the log heavy, then, we are actually describing not so much the log itself which we have not even touched, as the motor reactions which occur in our own bodies at sight of it. Perhaps we have never lifted any large log, so that there is no such exact experience for us to be reminded of; but we have certainly had many experiences with bulk and with density, whether we are actually aware of them at the moment or not, and the sight of this particular combination of bulk and density arouses in our musculature an approximate estimate of the weight of this particular log. Such an estimate, to be sure, has nothing to do with pounds and ounces for these are arbitrary, intellectually determined units adopted for convenience, and the muscles know nothing of them. Only the man who works habitually with scale divisions and has learned to associate the degree of muscular energy they stand for with various masses and densities will be able to make a fair guess of the weight of the log in pounds, but the rest of us will know at least how its weight compares with that of a stovepipe or a solid steel cylinder of equal dimensions.

All our perceptions are similarly matters of motor reaction. Otherwise they would not be perceptions at all, but mere sensations. Obviously, however, nobody who has lived in the world can have a simple sensation, for it must inevitably arouse associations with other sensations and the actions resulting from them. Thus when we find qualities in objects, such as hard and soft, rough and smooth, loud and faint, near and far, bright and dim, hot and cold, sweet and sour, square and round, high and low, we are actually describing the motor patterns which are set up in us by contact with such objects. If any object is broken down into its constituent elements, it will reveal the presence of no such ingredient as squareness or highness or hardness for these are qualities that do not constitute any part of the object itself but exist only in our experience of it. It would be nearer the truth to say that the squareness, the highness, the hardness, are in us, for they are essentially the names we give to neuromuscular experiences. If it were not for the presence of these movement-sense receptors throughout the body, constantly registering our postural changes and general movement activity, there would be no such thing as a smooth or a soft or a heavy object in the world, for nobody would be capable of distinguishing qualitative differences and everything would consequently appear to be exactly alike. Far more serious consequences than this would follow as well, to be sure, but in so far as aesthetics is concerned this would be serious enough.

Mere perception, however, is not the whole story of our relation to objects by any means, for there are also involved, besides the action we take or are prepared to take toward them, our feelings about such action which we call broadly emotion. Logically enough, the sense organs which report movement and postural change are closely connected with that part of the nervous system which belongs primarily to the inner man where emotions are generated. It follows naturally, then, that every emotional experience tends to make what we might call records of itself in motor patterns, setting up more of those well-worn paths in the neuromuscular system and adding new phases to those already set up. Thus in the rich storehouse of associations which life is always replenishing for us, the pathways from incoming sense impressions to the outgoing movements made in response to them lead through the territory of the inner man, and accordingly acquire for themselves inseparable emotional connotations. Our contact with an object, therefore, does not consist merely of recognizing it for what it is, but includes also an awakening of our feelings toward it. We live in a constant stream of emotional reactions, greeting every object, every situation, with favor or disfavor in varying degrees, reviving memories of previous experiences over the same neuromuscular paths, and making movements or preparations for movement according to the resultant of all these sources of testimony.

"Inner Mimicry"

PERCEPTIONS of objects affect us even more intimately than this, however, for it is virtually impossible for us to resist translating what we see or hear into our own present and active experience. To take a common example, when we see some one sucking a lemon we are more than likely to feel a distinct activity in the mouth and throat just as if it were we who were tasting the acid. When we look at bloodshot eyes, our own eyes are likely to water; if somebody yawns, we yawn; if somebody laughs, we laugh; if somebody cries, we frequently feel a lump rising in our own throats. If it were not for this propensity for experiencing synthetically whatever is presented to us, we should very often fail to understand the situation in which we chanced to find ourselves. When, for instance, we see signs of anger or rage in another, we are able to recognize them as such only because we have experienced them ourselves. Translating them automatically into a memory of these personal experiences, we understand at once the state of mind they represent and have warning to protect ourselves against a possible outburst of temper directed against us. Signs of fatigue in another are translated into a sympathetic awareness in our own bodies, and all types of gesture and facial expression convey meaning to us automatically because we have felt similar muscular experiences ourselves and recognize the postural attitudes and their emotional connotations as having happened to us.

Nor is this true only of our relations to other persons; it applies to impersonal objects as well. If we look at a building with columns supporting a mass above, we shall form a definite opinion as to whether the proportion is good or bad according to whether the mass that is supported seems easily supportable by the columns in question or too heavy for them. This reaction has nothing to do with any knowledge of architecture; it is a motor response. The building becomes for the moment a kind of replica of ourselves and we feel any undue strains as if they were in our own bodies. The reaction is exactly the same as the familiar sympathetic muscular strain we feel when we watch some one lift a tremendous weight or carry a staggering burden. "It makes me ache to watch him!" is the customary phrase for it, and the ache is present whether the "him" happens to be a person or an inanimate object. A sense of this sympathetic motor response to the function of the architectural column must have played some part, conscious or unconscious, in the mind of the designer of the Erechtheum when he caused one of its

porches to be supported by the figures of maidens, thus presenting the supporting force as actually occurring in the human
body. What an agonizing building it would have been if he
had made the maidens too small or the mass they had to bear
too heavy! A column not so suggestively personalized is only
slightly less productive of motor response in the onlooker, and
the same principle is at work in all our relations to architecture.

This faculty for transferring to our own consciousness those
motor experiences which an inanimate object before us would
undergo if it were capable of undergoing conscious experiences,
has been aptly termed "inner mimicry." It rarely results in very
clear outward or visible action, though it is true that we tend
to elongate the body when we look at a tall building or tower
and to spread ourselves broadly and comfortably before a low,
wide structure. Inwardly, however, we respond with vigor.
Psychologists have discovered changes in the postural condition
of the muscles in response even to shapes, though there is no
outward movement of any kind visible.

When reduced to theoretical statement, all this sounds a little
strange and perhaps even esoteric, yet it is simple and eminently
familiar in practice. We indulge in it every time we resort to
gesture to fill in verbal lapses, when we use our hands to
describe objects, or almost literally re-enact an incident we are
trying to tell. When we were children most of us have at one
time or another assumed a careful look of innocence and asked
an unsuspecting victim to tell us what a spiral staircase is, only
to burst into laughter when he has immediately resorted to
making descriptive circles in the air with his hand, as we had
known all along that he would do.

Again, if a large rock is seen on the ground with its longest
dimension parallel to the earth, it will almost inevitably be
described as lying on the ground, but if the same rock happens

to have its longest dimension extending into the air, it will be described as standing. This is a natural translation of the rock's position into that of our own bodies under similar circumstances. When a child bumps himself against a chair, it is a favorite device of parents to persuade him that the chair was hurt, also, and to induce him to rub its bruises. All this immediately suggests the animism of our primitive ancestors, and makes it clear that animism was no chance development but grew out of functional premises. It also provides a clearer understanding than any number of scholarly tomes could do of the close relationship that can exist between man and his environment, as well as between his religion, his art and his daily life.

We are continually attributing our own actions and reactions to the objects about us, and as a result the idiom of daily speech is so full of verbs of action used with inanimate subjects that the dictionaries record the usage as accepted. Hills roll and mountains rise, though they are perfectly stationary; the rolling and the rising are activities in us when we look at them. The wind howls and whistles shriek, because those are what we would call our actions if we were producing similar sounds. Examples are innumerable on every hand of the ease with which we personify the things about us.

There is an old joke about a farmer who found his lost horse by putting himself in the horse's place and just letting himself go naturally where the horse would go under the circumstances. This is an excellent formula for finding things even more elusive than a lost horse. If we want to "find" the Washington Monument or the Taj Mahal, Niagara Falls or the Grand Canyon, in terms of experience, we must do exactly as the farmer did, and have a similar imaginary transference of personality, so to speak. If we want really to "find" a Beethoven symphony we must hear it as our own voice with its emotional cadences and timbres, its breath phrase, pulse beat and body rhythms, arranged in the orderly utterance of a great experience and extended to a range far beyond that of ordinary life. To listen to it for its formal structure or its instrumentation is to have perhaps an intellectual pleasure in it but to miss its compulsive import and its essential vitality. We must *become* reflexively the Discobolus, the Mona Lisa, Hedda Gabler, Siegfried. It is because we are built with a central spine that we require of a painting that its masses balance about a central axis. Strict bilateral symmetry is perhaps too literal to be interesting, but too great a departure from it gives rise to an uncomfortable feeling of lopsidedness.

It is useless to approach any work of art with the notion that it must be understood before it can be responded to. Understanding is a process of rationalization after the experience; first there must be the experience or there is nothing to rationalize about. This all-important experience is to be gained in no better way than by following the old farmer's example.

From what has been said about the perception of objects as a motor function, it will be seen that there is a duality of approach involved. We were dealing a few pages back with a log across the path whose weight was sensed by looking at it, and a bit later with a stone whose implied action of standing or lying was judged by a translation of its "experience" into ourselves. The perception of any object has both these aspects inseparably; on the one hand we are concerned with what it is and on the other with what it is doing. This must inevitably follow since every object that has being has also an implication of action; if it is doing nothing more vigorous, it is at least standing or lying or sitting or spreading or rising or waving or flowing—or something of the sort.

Qualitative and quantitative attributes we know through contacts made by those senses which report on the outside world and through the motor patterns set up by these contacts. Action, on the other hand, we recognize only through having experienced it in ourselves. In the first instance, that of the log, we regard the object as a thing totally apart from ourselves with which we may have to deal in some indicated way. In the second instance, that of the stone, we identify ourselves with the object in a degree, in that we are aware of its state of action only in terms of our own experience of it; we look out from it, in a sense, instead of looking merely at it.

In daily life, where perception is an automatic function, the interoperation of these two processes takes care of itself naturally and easily. In art, however, where perception is in a certain degree a conscious process, we are more than likely to concentrate our attention upon the qualitative, the static element, leaving the vital factor of action virtually unperceived. That this does untoward things to the response to any work of art is evident, but what it does in the case of the dance is injurious beyond measure.

Response to the Dance

THUS far, little or nothing has been said directly about the response to the dance, for that, as must be clear by now, is potentially the simplest of all art responses. When the dancer appears on the stage, he presents to us movement of the human body, the very element in which we live. It is manifestly impossible, as we have seen, for him to make any movement which has not been either submitted to the inner man for his approval or dictated by him in the first place. In other words, the dancer's movements must inevitably have emotional connotations; he cannot make any other kind of movements unless his nervous system is pathological. (Even when movement is pathological, a tic or some other form of motor uncontrol is likely to appear grotesque because of its apparent implications of meaning quite inappropriate to the situation.) No movement of the human body is possible without definite relation to life experience, even if it is random or inadvertent.

Since we respond muscularly to the strains in architectural masses and the attitudes of rocks, it is plain to be seen that we will respond even more vigorously to the action of a body exactly like our own. We shall cease to be mere spectators and become participants in the movement that is presented to us, and though to all outward appearances we shall be sitting quietly in our chairs, we shall nevertheless be dancing synthetically with all our musculature. Naturally these motor responses are registered by our movement-sense receptors, and awaken appropriate emotional associations akin to those which have animated the dancer in the first place. It is the dancer's whole function to lead us into imitating his actions with our faculty for inner mimicry in order that we may experience his feelings. Facts he could tell us, but feelings he cannot convey in any other way than by arousing them in us through sympathetic action.

Obviously it is not the dancer's, or any other artist's, purpose simply to arouse us to feel emotion in a general sense, to stir us up to no end. It is his purpose, rather, to arouse us to feel a certain emotion about a particular object or situation. He wants to change our feeling about something, to increase our experience, to lead us from some habitual reaction which he has discovered to be perhaps merely inertia or otherwise limited and restrictive, to a new reaction which has an awareness of life in it and is liberating and beneficent. It becomes necessary for him, therefore, to do considerably more than just to work himself up into an excited emotional state and hop about in response to the whim of the moment. He must organize his material so that it will induce those specific reactions in us that will communicate his purpose. Only thus can he reveal to our experience the new reaction he has had and wishes us to have toward some particular object or situation.

An important part of his task is to make sure that he presents to us a clear grasp of this object or situation itself as well as of the state of feeling it arouses in him. The latter without the former tells us nothing, however much it may benefit the dancer by releasing his pent-up emotional energy. With the desire for communication, then, there comes the necessity for form and the beginning of art. This is a subject that requires discussion by itself.

Meantime, there remains an apparent contradiction to be reconciled. At the beginning of this chapter it was stated that the dance was perhaps the least generally grasped of all the arts, and now it is maintained that response to the dance is the simplest of all art responses. The two statements are both true and are brought into relation to each other by a third statement, previously made, to the effect that our total reaction to a work of art depends upon the equipment we bring to bear upon it, our past experience and present expectation. There is no disposition here to claim that the average spectator approaches the dance with anything but a perfectly functioning neuromuscular system and an equally healthy general physical organism, nor can there be any doubt that he has a wealth of associational material to serve as background. Where the difficulty is usually to be found is in the matter of his present expectation. He goes to a dance performance looking perhaps for storytelling, or musical rhythms, or sex appeal, or with almost any expectation except that of motor response. Obviously, under these conditions it is all but impossible for the dancer to make an impression on him.

Music would function no better if we did not listen to it. If we were to go to a symphony concert to concentrate on making a diagram of the conductor's arm movements, or to keep count of the total number of musical beats in each composition, or perhaps to study the walls and furnishings of the hall with an eye to redecoration, the best music in the world would become nothing but meaningless noise.

Painting would be similarly ineffectual if we looked at it merely to count the number of different colors, estimating the area of each and computing its proportion to the total area of the canvas. Here we should be using the correct and indeed the only visual instruments, but receiving no impression at all of the work of art. A great many people go through life totally insensitive to architecture because they see only a door here, a window there, and enough wall space between to place the grand piano against. They, too, are looking with the proper organs but they are seeing nothing at all of architecture.

It is essential when approaching the dance to carry along the expectation of response to movement and a reliance on the faculty of "inner mimicry." Because this is likely to be a new idea, it sometimes proves difficult at first; there is so much curiosity in the functioning of the "inner mimicry" itself that it often becomes the object of complete concentration. In that case it ceases to function, of course, and the dance goes by all but unnoticed. A bit of practice and persistence, however, will inevitably rectify this overenthusiasm for watching the wheels go round, and the dance will begin to function as an art of movement.

Chapter Two

FORM AND COMPOSITION

❧❧❧❦❦❦

FOR all the tremendous importance of form, the spectator needs to know remarkably little about it in order to enjoy a full and rewarding experience of art. Only when formulas are encountered is there need for any special knowledge, and then, it is true, the spectator must be something of a connoisseur. Normally, however, it is the business of the artist alone to bother about the laws of form and the solution of problems of composition; the spectator is concerned with nothing but the result. It is up to him to approve or disapprove, to accept or reject the finished work that is presented to him, on the basis of the reactions that are set up in him, and it is not his province to worry about how the reactions were achieved.

There is no other aspect of the arts about which so much nonsense has been talked, and none that has been transformed into such a hobgoblin to frighten away the layman. Form, to be sure, demands of the artist a knowledge of his materials and a skill in their manipulation, but it does not become thereby a matter of academic pedantry. Similarly, it requires intuition and sensibility of the highest order, but this does not place it in the realm of mysticism. Yet cults of form of both the academic and the mystical varieties flourish in all the arts, and increase incal-

26

culably the chasm between the artist and his rightful audience. Actually every normal adult is supplied by nature with all he needs in the way of equipment to react to form. This consists simply of the mechanisms of inner mimicry, motor response and association.

Form is not a separate entity, and cannot exist apart from materials. Like size or weight it is only an aspect of an object. Except as a useful term for philosophical speculation, "pure" form is as fantastic a concept as "pure" size or "pure" weight, and can exist no more in art than in nature. In so far as the definition of form is concerned, there is no difference at all between the form of a work of art and that of a chair or a door or an ocean liner, or for that matter, of a man or a tree or a horse. In any case, the purpose of form is the shaping of material so that it fulfills a specific function, and the resultant form itself is the particular disposition of elements thus arrived at by which the whole becomes something more than merely the sum of its parts.

A chair is not merely so many pieces of wood, it is something to sit upon; a door makes possible the closing and opening of an entry at will, and is therefore something quite different from a mere assemblage of boards. To be sure, some chairs and some doors are better formed than others, though all may perform adequately the function that makes them respectively chairs and doors. Workmanship that considers the most comfortable height and pitch of a chair seat, or the easy hang of a door on its hinges, undoubtedly produces better-formed objects. A heightening of form, and subtly of function as well, is obtained merely by the employment of pleasing proportion, by the arrangement of lines and masses so that a comfortable sense of balance and generally harmonious adjustments are aroused. As consumers we do not have to be instructed as to which object is the better; if we are insensitive and do not mind physical discomfort, the less well-formed objects will perhaps serve us satisfactorily, but mere contact with the better-formed will in all likelihood increase our immediate demands and raise our ultimate standards. Only if the door has a secret mechanism, however, or the chair must be sat in at a certain angle, shall we have to have any instruction regarding their functions and consequent desirability.

With art the situation is identical. The separate elements of which a work is composed must be held together in such a way that a unified experience, a total meaning, will result which would not otherwise exist. Three major considerations control the procedure of the composer. He must obviously have in mind the function for which his work is designed, he must know what materials to choose and how to handle them, and he must be aware of the mechanism of response in his audience in order not to overtax or understimulate it. Again, it is precisely the same procedure as that which directs the chairmaker. He does not take a casual armful of boards and sticks and play with them until he has put them together in some accidental fashion; he determines in advance what the end result is to be and is therefore not faced with the necessity of figuring out some purpose for the object once he has made it. Secondly, he knows better than to employ materials with such unsuitable modes of behavior as, say, tissue paper or wax for this purpose, and understands how to manipulate in the most efficient way the pieces of whatever material he does select. Thirdly, he does not make the legs of his chair four feet high, or its seat six inches wide; he is guided by his knowledge of the anatomical structure of the man who is to sit on the finished object.

The artist is likely to employ improvisation to some extent in the development of his composition, but he starts out with as clear a sense of the goal as the chairmaker does. Though he is generally not aware in advance of the details of the process, he knows the specific function for which his work is designed. This may vary over a wide range, from the conveying of a deeply stirring emotional truth to nothing more than the presentation of colors, lines and masses in arrangements calculated only to arouse a feeling of pleasant and orderly being, but its minimum function is the transference of an emotional experience of some kind and degree to the spectator. If it does less than this, it is not a work of art no matter how many facts it may state, events it may report or rules of procedure it may obey.

There is an element of compulsion about artistic creation that takes care in advance of the aim and purpose of any particular work, so that this does not become a matter for debate and selection. But the remaining factors, which involve the materialization of this compulsive inspiration—namely, the knowledge of materials and their behavior, and the judgment of the capacity for response that the spectator can be counted upon to possess— are less definitely indicated in advance. By the reconciliation of these three elements, however, the ultimate form of any work of art is determined. This reconciliation is effected largely by the method of trial and error, for composition is not a science in spite of the fact that there are pedagogues who try to teach it as if it were. Academic formulas have been devised from time to time only to be proved barren, since every work of art makes its own requirements as to form and there are no ready-made containers into which the substance of the artist's vision may be poured and still retain its individual force and character.

It is necessary at the outset to distinguish clearly between organic form and arbitrary forms. Organic form is that relationship of elements by which a self-determined identity is created with an inherent function emanating from the interoperation of its constituents, each of which is indispensably related to the whole. Arbitrary forms are arrangements of materials according to patterns agreed upon for reasons outside the inherent functions of the materials themselves.

In primitive art, for example, we sometimes find motifs repeated four, or eight, or nine times, according to whichever number happens to be sacred to the tribe. This is an entirely extraneous basis for form, but one that gives satisfaction to those who know and accept it. In more intellectual societies arrangements such as the rondel, rondeau, ballade and sonnet were invented and developed by rhetoricians equally without organic basis, and these, too, give pleasure to those with sufficient special knowledge to be able to accept them as basic forms. Pleasure in arbitrary forms is always less a matter of natural response than of specific training, and because of this, the subject of form in art often resolves itself in the popular mind into the learning and observance of formulas. Certain patterns are evolved in every period which become fashionable for a while and pass out of use, but the principle of organic form is the same now as it was in the earliest days of prehistory.

The application of this principle in the actual process of composition involves intuition and that faculty for self-criticism without which an artist can never hope to compose. Even in the midst of the most inspired moments of creativeness, the real artist is aware that a certain portion of himself is standing apart, passing judgment in the capacity of spectator. The artist who lacks this percentage of objectivity, who "loses himself in his art," is reasonably sure to leave his audience equally lost in it, though not in the same rapturous and intoxicated way. On the other hand, the composer who intellectualizes and analyzes his methods too closely is likely to find his productions stillborn.

The Character of Materials

AT the moment, however, ·the purpose is not to look at the subject of composition through the eyes of the composer in the throes of giving form to his inspirations, but rather to peer over his shoulder at the array of problems confronting him. If he were ever to see them spread out thus coldly before him in all their range and complexity, he would probably flee in terror from the prospect of having to master them. He works, however, from within his medium and allows it to carry him along to a large extent; he does not stand coldly outside it and manipulate it intellectually. For those of us, however, who wish to have some quite impersonal conception of the elements involved in dance composition, a fairly detailed analysis of the behavior of materials and the appeal to spectator response-capacity can do no harm. Happily, as spectators we need have no practical dealings with them, and once our curiosity has been satisfied, can put the whole matter out of mind.

As in any other art or craft, the nature and behavior of materials in the dance amount to inherent laws. Though the dancer makes some use of music, costume, architecture, acting, the painter's sense of color in décor and lighting, and in a small way even poetry where his titles are concerned, the actual stuff in which he works is movement.

All motion exists in the three dimensions of space, time and dynamics, and these must be considered not alone in their separate characters but also in the fusions and overlappings which give rise to such secondary phenomena as rhythm and phrasing, sequence and counterpoint. First, however, it is necessary to realize that dance employs a particular type of motion which affects all calculations. An inanimate object may be in motion if it is dropped or hurled or pushed, but the dance deals with the animate human body, not merely tossed about through the application of outside force, but in motion through its own volition. In other words, the body *moves,* whereas inanimate objects *are moved.* This obviously puts a definite color of motivation upon every phase of activity in any of the three dimensions of motion—upon direction, for example, and speed, and gradations of energy. Ultimately, it is true, all the other arts have similar demands to meet, and none of them can permit unmotivated and arbitrary lines, sounds, colors, masses. The dance, however, works in the most personal of all mediums, and the body that is seen making arbitrary and unmotivated movements is more than likely either to be unintelligible or to present a picture of insanity, since the normally co-ordinated human being does not make functionless movements in life. "Pure" form and "pure" line become therefore manifestly impossible in the dance, for in any movement or posture, however based merely on laws of design, there is bound to be an implication either of motivation or else of the inco-ordinations of mental unbalance.

This is perhaps the cardinal consideration in the approach to dance composition, namely, that movement of whatever kind carries within itself the implications of mood, purpose, function, emotion. The dancer does not work with an objective instrument like a piano or a palette of colors; he is himself the instrument. This makes it impossible for him to escape from connotations of the realism of human behavior, even though as a dancer he necessarily departs entirely from representationalism and all possible suggestion of pantomime. Thus, if he extends his leg so that his foot is higher than his head and sustains the position long enough (certainly an attitude without representational implications) he will most probably evoke applause from an audience; not because he has awakened any sense of abstract beauty by the obtuse angle he has formed, but because the muscular strain (a recognizable part of human behavior) which he has been able to withstand has surpassed normal endurance and his feat has been admired. The same thing will happen if he makes a great many turns at a great rate of speed, or performs any other series of extraordinarily rapid or manifestly difficult movements which in themselves are not expressive and might be counted on to function simply as elements of pure decoration or geometrics of motion. A succession of movements of this sort can become extremely exciting to an audience, by the evocation of sympathetic muscular experience, and it will sooner or later have to find a vent for its synthetically stirred-up state by shouting and beating its hands together. The niceties of pure aesthetic design, however, will have counted for little or nothing if, indeed, they have chanced to be present; the link exists in the connotations, however remote, of human behavior. The body is totally incapable of becoming an abstraction itself or of producing movement that is abstract in the sense of divorced from behavior.

It is easy to see how this situation affects the dance composer's dimensions of space, time and dynamics. His use of them is dictated first of all by the character of what he has to say and not by any extraneous principles of design. That there is another factor that tends to exert pressure upon him in the opposite direction we shall see in a moment, but it can safely be stated that the content of a work of art is the primary determinant of its form, just as water, sand, coal, milk and the uses to which they are to be put, determine the shape and texture of vessels suitable to contain them.

The dance is the only art that makes equal use of space, time and dynamics, but it is, of course, impossible to consider it as consisting of elements of space plus elements of time plus elements of dynamics, for they are not separable. It is possible, however, for the sake of analysis to consider the whole from the point of view of one of these aspects at a time.

Spatial problems have been treated most cavalierly by composers in general; it has frequently been thought quite enough to keep the face toward the audience and to balance a sortie to the right with a sortie to the left. Instinctively the better composers have discovered other and more respectable devices from time to time, but not until the advent of Rudolf von Laban with his theory, and more particularly Mary Wigman with her incomparable practice, was the subject of space given the attention it deserves.

By the dancer's prevailing awareness of the space in which and through which he moves, he relates himself consciously and visibly to his environment, and not only to the physical aspects of that environment but also to its emotional overtones. He places himself, as it were, in his universe, recognizing the existence of outside forces, benign and hostile. The dancer, on the other hand, who lacks this consciousness of the immediate world that surrounds him must necessarily concentrate on the exploitation of his person and his skills.

On this basis a wholly spectacular department of the dance has been built up, ranging from the bald exhibition of an ego in a vacuum to the development in the academic ballet of an exquisitely classic art. Following the line of classic practice in general, this departs by intention from the main stream of the dance as a biological phenomenon, so to speak, and sets up a self-contained existence upon the premise of an invented code of laws, quite unrelated to natural impulse and subjective experience and in no wise concerned with the illumination of man's relation to man or to his universe. Being thus cut off from the parent body of the dance, it is affected only in part by the operation of its laws. There is perhaps no more crucial point of division than that arising out of the spatial issue.

The pervasive presence of space, nevertheless, is the dancer's native realm, in much the same sense that air is the bird's or water the fish's, and it makes imperious demands upon both the performer and the composer. For the latter there is first of all the question of the amount of space to be employed and its character. Some compositions involve the extensive traversing of ground up to the utilization of the whole area available, while others unfold without change of base, that is, with the dancer remaining virtually in one spot. Because of the spatial values in the dance, stage setting and lighting assume a closer integrality with the composition itself than in other types of theatrical production. Here they do not serve merely as decoration or as descriptive place backgrounds, but take on the functional responsibilities of defining and delimiting the dancer's working area. Platforms, steps, ramps, pedestals and other structural forms are made to serve variously to break up a perhaps too monotonous expanse of merely empty stage with points of orientation, to afford areas where sheer height is available, to provide levels of contrasting elevation and different modes of access to them. Light can be used to restrict area and to increase it at will, to establish localized areas of different quality and accent, to cut off or to accentuate height, to blot out all tangible background and suggest limitless range.

These synthetic controls of space must, of course, be completely under the direction of the composer, who knows when he needs artificial elevation, points of orientation and constriction or expansion of working area. In the hands of stage designers working independently, they can become ruinous examples of mere visual ingenuity, impeding movement and throwing their own formal intentions athwart the dancer's design. The first important developments in this auxiliary branch of dance production were made in the years just before the World War by Appia, Salzman and Dalcroze in Hellerau, but little was done afterwards until Arch Lauterer turned his attention to the subject at the Bennington Festivals and produced for Hanya Holm's "Trend" in 1937 the first truly collaborative and functional stage setting for the dance to be seen in America.

But to return to the specific concern of the composer. Once the working area has been determined, there arise considerations of the possible disposition of the figure in the space available. It will achieve varying degrees of emphasis by being placed in the center of the area or at one side, forward or back; by clinging to the perimeter or by using the free body of the stage. In the matter of direction of movement, the forward and backward, the sideward, the diagonal, the curvilinear path, the broken line of progress, the turn in place, the shift of direction, all have definite values of their own.

Then there are the manifest differences of implication in the vertical aspects of the body—when it is seated or kneeling or lying on the ground, when it is crouching or stooped, when it is upright, when it is elevated upon the toes, when it is leaping into the air, and when it is falling. None of these things is a matter of free choice or pure invention for the creative choreographer, but will evolve for him in the main out of inner impulsion.

Also touching in a measure upon the category of space problems is the consideration of whether the movement of the individual is simple, as when the entire body unites in the performance of a single action, or complex, as when parts of the body move in opposition to each other. When this essential problem is increased in dimensions, with different dancers, instead of different parts of the same body, working in opposition to each other, there can be no question that space problems are involved, for here we have a definite instance of spatial counterpoint. With a composition involving more than one dancer, all space relations are intensified. Aside from the subtleties and the selective aspects of composition, it becomes necessary at once to guard against such major dangers as simple confusion in which some figures interfere with the activity of others and nothing emerges with clarity. It is manifestly impossible to move a stageful of dancers always in uniform mass, and the evolving of simultaneous patterns in space necessitates the careful maintenance of relationships so that emphasis falls only where it should for the adequate development of the central plan. The cardinal issue here is how much the spectator can be counted upon to perceive; and of that, more later.

All these problems of space involve elements of time as well, for manifestly it is impossible to move through space without occupying time. Thus the number and variety of impressions made by spatial conduct are increased in geometrical progression by the added consideration of their time aspects.

With such elementary matters as speed and slowness, gradual accelerations and retardations, or sudden shifts in the rate of movement there are no bewilderments. It is when we approach more complicated involvements in which time and dynamics are concerned together that difficulties appear. This is the category in which the vexed subject of rhythm exists, with its corollaries, phrasing and sequential development. Indeed, as soon as rhythm is mentioned, we are likely to find ourselves enveloped in as dense a fog of mysticism and vagueness as that which beclouds the subject of form itself.

It is wise when considering rhythm in the dance to put aside all preconceptions deriving from musical rhythm. The latter, it is true, originates at the same source, namely, the natural movement of the body, but as music has been developed as an absolute art, its relation to bodily experience has become increasingly attenuated until in many instances it approaches the point of disappearance.

All rhythms are products of dynamics, concerned only incidentally with time. They consist basically of the alternations of accent and unaccent; the time element enters only with the periodicity of the alternations.

Bodily rhythms are made up of the successive contractions and relaxations of muscles. The most persuasive of them, because they are continuous, organic, generally regular, and above all, because we are aware of them, are the pulse of the blood and the process of breathing. Against these as a background, we are inclined subconsciously to measure all other rhythms, phrasings and tempos.

Walking, hammering and similar repetitive activities are readily seen to be rhythmic successions of contractions and relaxations, fairly simple in character. Any movement is rhythmic, however, even though there is not such a marked contrast between its strong and weak elements, if it maintains a comfortable alternation of contractions and relaxations. It is not necessary for the two elements to be of equal duration, for this is frequently not the case even in movements that appear to be regular, like breathing.

Rhythm in the dance, being merely a concentrated adaptation of the rhythms of the body, is similarly based on alternation and recurrence, but it need not therefore be the monotonous succession of single units like the action of hammering. Once the presence of a periodic dynamic alternation has been established, almost limitless variations may be played upon it. The pattern of each variation may then be set up as a larger rhythmic unit in itself, namely, the phrase, to be subjected in turn to alternation and recurrence. Variations, to be sure, cannot be arbitrary, for it is perhaps necessary to repeat that the dancer cannot dodge the responsibility for setting up implications of function and intention by whatever he does. The larger rhythmic unit, the motor phrase, must therefore have some organic logic about its development. If the motor phrase were subjected to definition it would probably be described as a succession of movements from a common impulse, not necessarily sufficient to constitute a complete statement of action but containing either the introduction of a theme or a response to such a theme already introduced.

To illustrate, it might consist, let us say, of some such elements as a sequence of steps to the front ending with one foot raised, while the arms complete a wide circle upwards. Or perhaps in a more clearly functional manifestation, it might be made up of an initial movement which tends to throw the body out of equilibrium and those succeeding movements in the course of which equilibrium is restored. In any case, the series of movements would necessarily have a characteristic pulse, though they need not inevitably be evenly spaced or timed, and would possess a unity that set them apart from what had been done previously or what was to follow. This unity would be the natural outcome of the fact that the phrase was the result of a single impulse, a single motor idea, so to speak.

There is no prescribed length for a motor phrase nor any fixed regulation as to how much material it must contain. A complete statement of action comparable to a sentence in rhetoric or a period in music may demand several phrases, consisting not only of a subject and a response but perhaps also of the introduction of new subjects before the first has been resolved. The content of the projected work is the sole arbiter. Thus we are led at once into the matter of sequential development, and a composition is seen to be built up by the juxtaposition of motor phrases.

In dance rhythms and phrases, time will play the smallest conscious part, and the spectator will be aware of them chiefly in terms of recurrent spatial patterns with dynamic variations. Dynamism, indeed, is the heart and soul of rhythm and the vitalizer of the whole art. All movements exist between the extremes of complete tension and complete relaxation, and dance composition concerns itself accordingly not only with the distribution of movement through space and time, but also with the amount of movement to be utilized. As music consists of a continuous stream of sound—punctuated by brief pauses and modified in pitch, speed and intensity, but still a continuous stream—so dance consists of a continuous stream of movement, similarly modified. Spasmodic bursts of movement scattered through space no more constitute a dance than separate bits of marble scattered through space constitute a sculpture. A unity of substance, a continuum, so to speak, is required, which in the dance consists of a sustained muscular tone, a heightened dynamic state, which is never allowed to lapse, though it is constantly varied, until the dance is over.

This dynamic continuum is primarily a matter of quantity determining whether dance movement exists at all and in what degree, but its variations constitute that aspect of movement which we call quality. In the field of comparative intensities lie all increases and diminutions of force, all degrees of sharpness of attack, rigidity and fluidity, gradations of accent and unaccent, flexions, extensions, and rotations, leaps and falls, devitalization and rest.

Demands of the Spectator

So much for the subject of the materials of dance and their behavior; now to consider the manipulation of them in such a fashion that a finality is achieved and the spectator is left with a sense of satisfaction.

Experience of spectator response through many generations has made certain methods of procedure virtually mandatory, not by academy decree, but for functional reasons discovered by the painful trial-and-error system. Many of them, though perhaps not all, are commonplaces, for though we have not all been composers, we have all been on the receiving side of the process innumerable times, and our demands, whether we have made them overtly or not, have been along well-defined lines.

It is the composer's responsibility to capture the attention, hold it on the basis of climactic building of interest, and release it only with the culmination of his project, making sure that the release will have in it sufficient compensation for the expenditure of energy demanded up to this point. A beginning must be made simply and relationships between various thematic elements established gradually. To be thrust at once into a complicated situation is rather like opening one's eyes in a maze with nothing to suggest the way out.

It is of the utmost importance to indicate the path of progress step by step in advance. Unfamiliar material is far more difficult to follow than familiar, and must therefore be carefully prepared for and anticipated. If it is completely strange and unexpected, it is likely to produce no effect whatever, like words spoken in an unknown language. On the other hand, if it is too familiar, the response is likely to be almost mechanical and require so little effort of the attention that the mind will be allowed to wander off to more exciting fields. The problem then is to provide enough novelty to keep the interest, but to build on a groundwork of reasonable familiarity and with due preparation. The unknown, as in any type of activity, must be couched in terms of the known. Continuity—which is only another way of saying a cleared path for the attention—is attained simply by preparing for each successive step within the preceding one, so that when it arrives it has a comfortable enough feeling of familiarity about it to support that element which is new. Even those elements which are planned for surprise must be prepared for, at least to the extent of a warning to expect the unexpected.

The first preparation is made by the title, which in effect sets the stage before the work begins. It may indicate the subject matter of what is to follow, or the mood in which it is to be cast, or something of its pattern, any of which is helpful in establishing a point of contact. A poor title or a vague one often seriously hampers a dance composition by leading the expectation into the wrong channels. The title is, of course, no part of the work itself, but an extraneous device to facilitate its reception by setting up certain associations that can be built upon when the composition gets under way. Thus the basis for continuity is established even before the opening phrase.

Continuity in itself is obviously not enough to insure attention, any more than the sight of a cleared road is an irresistible lure to travel it irrespective of its destination and the scenery by the wayside. Along with continuity, a state of expectancy must be maintained and its fulfillment ever promised but ever postponed. This quality of suspense may rely merely on the natural urge for the completion of an act begun, or it may be heightened by the introduction of a counterelement which tends always to turn the act away from its logical completion and is not conquered until the last moment. Devices to prolong the state of unfulfillment serve to increase the pleasure of the final resolution by increasing the vigor and insistence of the demand. The process is not unlike that of hunger, in that the longer food is delayed or the more the appetite is increased by such synthetic devices as cocktails, the greater the pleasure in the eating and the larger the amount that can be consumed. The experience of hunger is not in itself a pleasant one, to be sure, and if there is no guarantee of food ahead it can become an exceedingly painful one, but the natural unpleasantness of the experience can be completely transformed by the anticipation of pleasurable fulfillment.

In art it is possible for us to extend the range of our experience into unpleasantnesses which in life we must avoid, because we have always ahead of us the assurance of a pleasurable resolution, and hence a much sharper experience of pleasure than the mere level routine of safe living can provide. In its use of suspense, art provides us with an extension of experience into the enthralling realm of danger, with the certainty of complete safety. To be harrowed and wracked—within limits, of course—becomes not painful but pleasant with the anticipation of a proportionate recompense. To be sure, not all art is as dramatic and emotionally stirring as this, but even if the issue is no greater than the threatened incompletion of an aesthetic design, the fringe of adventure has been touched.

Aside from the consideration of familiarity and unfamiliarity, some material is easier of reception than other. Because it is the nature of the organism to defend itself against inharmonious adjustments and to invite harmonious ones, that material is most easily effective which awakens pleasurable associations. The clear, bright color, the soft tone, the gentle modulation, the curved line, the smooth and even-flowing movement, invite no resistance, whereas the discordant tone combination, the angular line, the irregular rhythm, the abrupt attack, arouse defensive and even avertive reactions and conflicting adjustments. The work of art, therefore, which wins the most widespread popularity is the one which deals in materials of the easiest reception.

Those works, however, which have the most momentous consequences in art and in the redefining of human values are always those which require the receptive consciousness to extend itself beyond these rather lazy boundaries. By demanding unfacile adjustments and the resolution of irregular and antagonistic combinations, they compel an extension of the grasp and practice of universal order. This has been true of every important work (though not every popular work) in the history of art, and a means of extending the range of art both in the depth of human values and in technical mastery from generation to generation. This is not to be attributed to any deliberate intention of the artist to be moralistic or educational, but simply to the fact that as an artist he is more sensitive to his environment than the majority of those about him and is faced first with the necessity for making new adjustments.

In the handling of thematic material, repetition, up to the point where it becomes monotonous, is increasingly pleasurable, providing an opportunity for recognition both of what has been previously presented and of its manner of presentation. When a phrase or a complete statement is brought into play a second or a third time, it travels over a path already cleared but not traversed so often as to have become virtually automatic. On the basis of repetition, variations may be introduced, relying on the familiarity of the material to sustain them, and even to make them doubly pleasurable because of a comfortable margin of novelty and an element of contrast. The pleasure of repetition is also increased if in the meantime material of another character has been introduced, for, again, contrast heightens the intensity of the recognition.

Responses, however, like muscles, are subject to fatigue. Persistence on a single theme produces ennui just as readily as the overtaxing of a single muscle. Endurance of interest is lengthened if there is a wider distribution of attack, always with the proviso that the spread is not so great as to produce a sense of disunity.

This spread may involve not only alternation and variation of theme in sequence, but may also consist of presenting simultaneous themes or basic movement materials too large to be performed by a single dancer. As a rule it is easier to sustain attention with the unified activity of a group of dancers than it is with a single figure, for there is a wider field of interest and less necessity for close concentration; but it is above all essential that such activity shall be unified. Attention is lost if it is required to focus on more than one thing at a time. If two things occur simultaneously in a composition they must either be so related as to become virtually one or else so arranged that one is comparatively negligible—perhaps a mere marking of time or else the continuous repetition of a simple theme of moderate accentuation which can be easily registered as a background for more striking action. Because of differences in the processes of seeing and hearing, musical harmony and counterpoint are considerably freer in range and can indulge in greater elaborations than their spatial equivalents, for visual objects do not blend as sounds do. Whether this is due in part to lack of experience in looking at spatial counterpoint or altogether to essential differences in the respective powers of the eye and the ear to focus is for the psychologists to say.

Even with a broader attack, however, it is necessary, in order to sustain vigor of response, that greater and greater stimulation be provided as the work progresses. A simple beginning is indicated, therefore, not only because it is difficult for the spectator to grasp an involved one, but also because it is difficult to build upward from a starting point that is already high.

Musical Forms

THUS far what has been discussed has obviously more relation to the elements of organic form and the compositional approach to its realization than to any particular dance forms. As a matter of fact, the dance is virtually free from predetermined forms. This was not always the case, and in primitive societies where rituals prevail, it is still not so. Nevertheless, in the art dance of the present time, the routine approach that so grieved Noverre in the eighteenth century and the reformers who came after him, no longer exists. The overturning which took place in the wake of Isadora Duncan destroyed the old stereotypes pretty effectively.

The dance today is singularly unfettered. There is nothing even approximately equivalent to the sonnet or the sonata, where a definite procedure is prescribed. Perhaps the nearest approach to it is the pas de deux which is still seen in the formal manner in revivals of nineteenth century ballets—and approximations of their style—that is, first, an adagio section in which the ballerina is exhibited by her partner; then a solo, called a variation, by each of them; and finally a coda in which they are together again, this time in allegro movements. Nowadays, however, even this term has lost its set meaning, and pas de deux signifies any dance for two, without formal restrictions.

Sometimes antique dances such as the sarabande, the courante, the galliard, the minuet, are referred to as dance forms, but this is a loose manner of speaking. Even in the days of their practice in the ballrooms of the nobles of the Renaissance and later, few if any of them were rightly to be considered as forms. Today, their choreographic aspects have been generally forgotten, and in the line of direct survival they have come down to us only through their musical influences. Music written according to the patterns of certain of them was employed in contrasting combination to make up the musical suite, but since this popular musical device long outlasted the dances on which it was patterned, it is only natural that it should have become thoroughly musicalized and progressively isolated from its source material. Actually it does little more than retain the characteristic rhythm phrases and the general spirit of the original dances.

The antique dances, particularly in the sketchy state in which we know them, are not to be considered in any sense as forms, therefore, but rather as rhythmic schemes, and step patterns, in much the same way that the waltz, the fox-trot, the tango, are rhythmic schemes, and step patterns. They are comparable not to such a self-contained form as the sonnet, but rather to the type of verse that characterizes it, that is, the iambic foot in a five-foot line. A form is necessarily a definitive structure with beginning and end, and is not to be confused with the details of design which it may employ. A room, for example, has form in that it demands a minimum number of surfaces in order to be a room; but the wallpaper which decorates it consists merely of a series of repeated units of design which may continue indefinitely. Any of these rhythmic schemes may be put into form by a composer if he chooses to employ them, but they do not constitute forms in themselves.

What accent there is on predetermined forms in the dance today is largely the effect of that dependence upon music which grew, as an inadvertent by-product, out of Isadora Duncan's practice, and which has not yet been totally overcome. Though

Isadora overthrew all the old choreographic formulas, she subjected the new and free substance of her dance to the influence of highly organized musical forms which completely dominated it structurally. In her published writings she has stated that her use of such music was no part of her theory but only an immediate personal necessity, since from no other source could she obtain the inspiration she required. By many of those who followed her, however, the superimposing of musical forms upon dance material was seized upon as a definite method and has continued in force to some extent ever since. This is true not only of those types of dance which obviously owe their beginnings to Isadora, but of the ballet as well. If the musical composer has already put his ideas into form, the dance composer apparently feels that he need not bother to do likewise but can lean instead upon the musician's work.

Logically enough, when the more progressive choreographer first sees the need for breaking away from this hampering dependence upon music, he is more than likely to take with him as his basis for independent composition those practices which he has automatically acquired from the musician. By reason of this inertia, it is the frequent procedure of dancers, even when composing entirely without the aid of music, to follow musical formulas, in spite of the fact that forms devised specifically to solve musical problems are generally unsuitable to dance.

The basic principles of organic musical form, to be sure, are at one with those of organic dance form and stem from the same root. Dance and music are extremely close and in their origins virtually inseparable. Dance without song or song without dance is a relatively late development, and then only in the Western world. An independent musical art exists nowhere else and an independent dance art is equally unthinkable. Manifestly, the man who is totally possessed by the impulse to externalize his emotional state will not omit any instrumentality at his command, and complete dance must involve voice as well as movement. If the dancer has insufficient breath for both, the song can be delegated to others. No matter who does the singing, however, it is always essentially the dancer's voice that is being represented, and this becomes no less pressing a necessity even after the song has evolved into wordless and orchestral music.

When the combination of dance and song is dissolved into its separate halves and each half goes its own way without regard for the original relationship, their higher individualistic developments become remote and irreconcilable. When they are put together again into a joint function, it is necessary to turn them back to that point near their common origin at which they began to part. Since music has been developed to a far higher degree in its own sphere, its realliance with dance entails a considerable sacrifice of purely formal musical progress. For this reason many musicians will not consent to write for dance because of the retrogression involved, and even more are unable to do so because of a widespread inability to grasp, in anything but theory, the original dance aspects of music with which they have had no personal contact.

Nevertheless, if the chief musical forms are examined, it will be seen that those few which are actually forms in the organic sense are as much dance forms as they are musical. Some of them are not even definitive entities but merely combinations and devices, and hence fall outside the classification of forms in spite of accepted usage.

The one-section type of composition, typified by some of the simpler folk songs and an occasional prelude by a more sophisticated composer, is, of course, equally applicable to short types of dance, and is an entirely organic manifestation of form, being merely a single complete statement of rhythmic action.

The two-section form is certainly as much a dance form as a musical. It is only a further extension of the essential base of rhythm; the next larger step after the balancing of phrases to make a section is the balancing of sections according to the same plan. In spite of its increased dimensions, it is still in effect a contraction followed by a relaxation—a statement and a response, a question and an answer. This is obviously founded on an organic principle, though the mere use of the letter of the device without regard for the inner relation of the material in the two sections is no guarantee that organic form will be realized.

The three-section form, commonly referred to as A-B-A, states a theme, follows with another of contrasting character, and repeats the first. There is, again, an inherent possibility of formal completeness in such a program of action, which belongs to the dance as well as to music and is frequently employed by it. There are innumerable implications possible in its use. For example, it is as if in the emphatic statement of a point the composer wishes to say: "This first statement is true; this second statement may also be true; but the important thing is that this first statement is true." Or perhaps, more dramatically, the first section makes a compelling statement, the second attempts to deny it, and the repetition of the first refutes the denial. Or again, it may be an enlargement of the two-section form for clarity and emphasis. To take an example from the nursery jingle: "What are little girls made of?" (First section.) "Sugar and spice and everything nice." (Second section.) "That's what little girls are made of." (Repetition, not only on a more positive basis, but also to point out that the recipe in the second section was not a mere digression but was strictly on the original subject.)

This form bears a close relation to the rondo, which is often

said to have grown out of it but which may just as logically
have given birth to it. The rondo consists of a single basic theme
followed by any number of other themes with a return to the
basic theme after each, as A-B-A-C-A-D-A, etc. Since there is no
limit to the numbers of themes that may be introduced, this is
manifestly not a definitive form. One of its early usages is in
the choral dance-song in celebration of the exploits of a hero,
in which the legend is told by a leader with periodic interrup-
tions by a group in a refrain. The form is completed when the
story is completed. Here it is actually the material that supplies
the definitive element. Another and perhaps slightly less extraneous manner of drawing the form to a conclusion is to be seen
in a type of ancient round in which the dancers circle in a
characteristic figure, and each dancer in turn takes the center to
perform a figure of his own. The whole is given shape of sorts
by the fact that the dance is not complete until every participant
has made his contribution. It is possible to consider the A-B-A
form as perhaps one man's share in such a dance as this—a
group figure, the emergence of a soloist, his return to the group.
Certain "longways" country dances employ something of the
same plan, each couple executing a figure in turn and rejoining
the entire company for a repetition of a general figure between.
Again, the end is determined in advance by the number of participants. It was in such a form as this that the early French
ballet and opera couched the inevitable grand chaconne of its
final act.

For the rest, there are no clean-cut organic claims to be made.
Sonata form is an elaboration of the two-section form, with
nothing at all inevitable about the manner in which it has been
elaborated. Changes in tonality play an important part that the
dance cannot possibly hope to parallel, and it is, indeed, a purely
musical development, with an arbitrary logic of its own, and

no organic structural basis. The sonata as a whole, consisting of several movements of which "sonata form" usually shapes only the first, is an outgrowth of the old dance suite, but nothing remains of the original except the contrasting character of the various movements, and frequently one movement in the pattern of the minuet.

The fugue, as Sir Donald Tovey has said of it, is "a texture rather than a form." Its end is in no wise implicit in its beginning; it may, indeed, run on forever, and in the hands of a composer only moderately skilled never acquire any aesthetic contours at all. It is not a form but a manner of procedure, its chief feature being the presentation of a leading theme or subject in each of a number of voices in turn, while the other voices continue with secondary material. Something in the nature of fugue or canon is frequently employed in the dance, as in certain longways dances in which each couple in turn performs a series of patterns introduced by the leading couple; but in dances designed to be seen by spectators, it is a device that can be used only incidentally and at some risk. Highly contrapuntal arrangements in any medium demand great mental concentration from an audience, and so much so in the dance that they are generally conducive of little besides visual confusion.

The theme with variations is not a specific form but rather a type of compound composition consisting of a number of individual forms. Each variation is a complete entity, and may be of virtually any type, while the whole is united by a common subject rather than by any structural unity. The varying of a theme is a widely used composing practice, whether in music or dance, but it does not constitute a definitive form, since it sets no limits for itself in either extent or procedure. Bach has employed as many as thirty variations in the Goldberg set, and Beethoven thirty-three in the Diabelli.

Music and dance are seen, thus, to have much in common along formal lines, but to be far from identical in their individualistic developments. Materials play so vital a part in the shaping of form that the application of any of these common principles to music and to dance produces quite different results, and there is actually no formal unity between them. The dancer, therefore, who takes any old rag-tag and bobtail of movement and depends upon its meticulous arrangement according to musical formulas to give it validity is doomed to failure from the start.

Doris Humphrey, a master of dance form, once gave a lecture in which she demonstrated all the standard procedures and formulas and concluded by remarking that though these were the accepted methods of composition, she herself never composed according to them. Her method, she said, was rather to let the central idea of a composition grow in her mind and eventually work itself out in a form of its own. Most mature artists, it is safe to say, work in some such manner, with the result that no handy compendium can be relied upon as a key to their creation, and to look always for musical form in them is virtually to insure missing the point.

Drama and Dance

In many respects, the dance is more closely related to drama than to music, though especially since the days of Isadora Duncan, emphasis has been otherwise directed. The dancer and the actor are actually the same person in slightly different guises, but the dancer and the musician very early become two persons, supplementary to each other and engaged in separate divisions of the same art.

The musician takes the experience of the dance and attenuates it into a disembodied emotion, so to speak, leaving the personal performance behind. The actor, on the other hand, retains the element of personal performance, but instead of attempting any rarefaction, makes it more inclusive and more specific. The dancer in his performance represents only himself as a type of the race reacting in the present moment to the world about him; the actor becomes a particular individual in a particular plot situation. Both employ movement as their medium, and each adds a characteristic sound equivalent. Where the sound equivalent for the dancer has the same broadly symbolic quality as his movement, that for the actor falls into the more specific forms of speech, varying in its literalness from highly exalted verse to colloquial prose.

The division between dance and drama becomes at times exceedingly fine; indeed, the greater part of the existing dance repertory leans well over the line. The moment the dancer ceases to appear as himself experiencing a present emotion, and assumes a character, he steps into the actor's field, though not necessarily into the range of dramatic form. When in addition he retails some exploit, real or imaginary, he invokes automatically that particular sequential arrangement which belongs to dramatic form. A vast majority of the larger dance works designed for the stage are equipped with both characterization of sorts and plot; and the latter, even though it may be little more than a thread upon which to string incidental dances, frequently provides the only structure by which any semblance of formal unity is attained.

Dramatic form as such can be said to exist when the dance, instead of presenting the essence of an emotional experience, deals with a specific sequence of events out of which such an experience grows. The more literal its treatment, the less it has of dance about it. The essential basis of dramatic form is reducible to the following simple formula: the presentation of a leading theme, the introduction of a countertheme in direct opposition to it, a clash between the two, and the emergence of one of them as victor. This is eminently applicable to certain types of dance composition, and can obviously be employed without resort to the kind of highly detailed plot and closely identified characterization that are required in storytelling. Dances of high emotional content but of less inclusive form normally deal with only the last of these sections, that is, with the summation of an emotional experience. Dances of more lyric character naturally eschew the dramatic form altogether.

Drama and dancé are seen even more strikingly as merely different levels of the same art when they are viewed at a point before the element of form properly enters into consideration at all. Composition, as the process of putting materials into form, concerns itself first necessarily with materials, and the basic stuff of drama and the basic stuff of dance are identical. The difference is altogether in the approach to it, for drama thinks of it as action and dance thinks of it as movement.

Frequently the young dancer, along with the uninspired among his elders, feels that he can rely upon musical principles for his forms, but has no notion where to turn for his choreographic materials, that is, for the movement which is the substance of his dance. Music, his habitual guide and support, can offer him no help here, having long since been developed away from any direct concern with bodily action. In his plight, he generally follows one of three courses: either he allows music to "inspire" him to improvise; or if perhaps he rightly mistrusts this reliance on suggestibility, he invents arbitrary movements that look "original" and uses them to fill in an objective pattern; or he simply arranges and rearranges old familiar movements without any thought whatever of creativeness of material.

The solution of his problem (unless, of course, he is dealing with a traditional type of dance with a rigidly determined vocabulary) lies in turning directly to the fact that the body reacts to all stimuli first in terms of movement, and that communicative movement suitable for dance can be drawn only from what might be termed his motor memory of emotion. He must learn how to call upon his emotional associations and translate them into action directly from life experience.

This is exactly the same fundamental problem that belongs to the actor's art, though the actor with his broader medium need not concentrate on sheer movement. This was the basis of Stanislavsky's discovery at the turn of the century by which, as director of the Moscow Art Theatre, he revolutionized theater practice. During those same years Isadora Duncan was discovering it to be the fundamental problem of the dancer's art, unrecognized since the days of antiquity, but more vital by far than any matters of form. Indeed, such matters were seen to be largely dependent upon the development of movement out of life experience.

Isadora has described in her autobiography her discovery of the origin of movement in the solar plexus, "the temporal home of the soul," and in this discovery, unscientific as it possibly is, she touched on the theory of movement evolved directly out of emotion which is the crux of the whole creative problem of the dance. Further, she tells of her efforts to discover a "first movement" based on a primary emotion from which a whole series of movements would flow as a kind of natural reaction without any mechanics of deliberate invention. Here is, indeed, the ideal pattern of the motor phrase. Such ideas were unheard of in the early nineteen hundreds, and are still far from being understood by the great majority of dance composers.

No movement sequence with the logic of emotion in it, however, is created by any other means, even though oftener than not it is only pure accident that produces an eloquent phrase. The fear of killing "inspiration" frequently prevents the tapping of the wellspring from which it flows, namely, experience seen in perspective. Certainly Stanislavsky's actors, with whom nothing was "inspirational" in the erroneous sense of improvisational, were never led into mechanical or routine performance by the application of the actor's approach to the same technic; it was that very thing, in fact, and nothing else, that saved them from mechanics and routine. Nothing else can perform a similar service for the contemporary dance, and put an end to the theory of excellence by accident as the only alternative to the three barren courses of action which prevail so widely in the dancer's approach to the discovery of his materials.

To be sure, highly personal emotional experiences cannot be taken in toto and put upon the stage as dances; they would be not only extremely embarrassing, as personal confessions always are, but also largely unintelligible because of their close relationship to the private and involved affairs of one individual's life. These experiences are only the ore from which the pure metal must be extracted, and the process of extraction is the most important element of dance composition and the one that makes the greatest demands on genius.

Here the actor and the dancer definitely part company, each to provide in his own way the necessary perspective by which personal experience is transformed into the stuff of art. The actor (or rather the dramatist who provides him with the composition he is to perform) turns to characterization. The emotional experience which is at the heart of the work is transferred to a fictitious personality, created synthetically from both inward and outward observation and endowed with such qualities that this experience can logically happen to him under a given set of fictitious circumstances. The element of personal confession is thus removed, since the surface that is presented is quite objective; the intricacy of personal detail is likewise eliminated by supplying only enough of such detail concerning the invented character to clarify the immediate situation, omitting the many extraneous complications which would attach to him if he were completely and naturalistically transcribed from life. Though he may give the impression of a fully rounded personality, he is, of course, nothing of the sort, for only that part of his life which has to do with one particular dramatic episode has been created. He has been greatly altered from the pattern of actuality in order to provide those emphases which the artist needs to make his point. Clearly Hecuba, Clytemnestra, Medea; Hamlet, Lear, Othello; Pantalone, Pierre Patelin, Tartuffe; Hedda Gabler, Paula Tanqueray, Salvation Nell; Rip Van Winkle, Simon Legree, Jeeter Lester—are all merely dramatic abstractions from life and not life itself.

To the extent that the dancer from time to time steps into this field of characterization, he employs the same method of abstraction. His characterization, however, is never as detailed as the actor's and usually is the characterization of a type rather than of an individual. When he is a warrior, he is never General So-and-so at the Battle of Such-and-such, but is the typification of all warriors; when he is a butterfly (which happily he is not impelled to be very often these days), or a peasant, or a hobgoblin, he is the typification of all butterflies, peasants and hobgoblins.

This also gives an inkling of his approach on the far more significant occasions when he is not adopting the actor's medium of characterization in any degree but is functioning purely as a dancer. Then he dances in his own person as the type of all men in contact with some emotional force. If he dances about war or death, spring or love, he does not personify them, but rather externalizes some new emotional insight into them which he wants the spectator to recognize as belonging potentially to himself and to all men.

Naturalistic gesture is immediately ruled out, for it is commonplace, personal and particular. The impulse behind gesture, however, is the kernel of the matter, for the urge to move in generally the same tone in response to the same stimuli is common to all men. Here we are on the threshold of a universal medium of communication. It remains only for this common impulse behind gesture to be materialized in the dancer's movement with such breadth of dimension and clarity of outline that it will awaken the spectator to recognition of its personal significance for him. Literal mimetics cannot accomplish this experience of identification, for they contain too much that is purely objective. The dancer's movements are abstract; that is, they have abstracted the essentials from a particular life experience, omitting all that is merely personal and without universal significance. If, for example, a dancer were to compose a dance of farewell, he would not feel called upon to insert wavings of the hand or tears or embracings of an imaginary partner. These are the external commonplaces of the situation and would not warrant the making of a dance at all. Just what he would feel called upon to do cannot be prophesied, for it would grow from a personal and inward illumination. His material, however, would be distinctly less superficial and more intuitive than these outward tokens, based on a keen inner realization of the emotional forces involved, and utterly unpredictable in detail.

Almost the only thing that can be said of any dance composition in advance is that it will definitely not be an exact or even an approximate reproduction of nature; it will certainly take nature as its base, but will reshape nature's forms so that the attributes which the composer is anxious to make clearer than they are in life will be magnified, and those with which he is not concerned will be minimized or eliminated. Sometimes this process results in a heightening of sensuous beauty, in which case it is likely to be considered as idealization; sometimes it results in quite the opposite state, in which case it is more than likely to be called distortion. The process, however, is exactly the same, and is inseparable from the business of composition. It is the process, indeed, which differentiates art from life, and makes possible the creation of that compensatory world in which art dwells.

Not all types of dance, to be sure, employ movement creatively in the manner here discussed. In spite of the fact that this is the root of the whole art, according to history as well as to internal evidence, in all periods and in all arts crystallizations of method and vocabulary occur which gradually grow so habitual for one reason or another that they become laws in themselves and tend to supersede creative experience as the point of departure for the artist. The controlling reasons for this are many, having to do with religious prescription, social caste, fashion, academism, and all the other monopolistic institutions of conservatism.

Such tendencies begin early in history in the notoriously conservative society of primitive peoples. When a dance with religious or social significance has become accepted as ritual, it is death to the dancer who changes the smallest detail of it. Thus dances are kept superficially alive from generation to generation even after their original purposes have been forgotten and the accompanying songs have degenerated into mere gibberish through constant but uncomprehending repetition.

In many parts of the world, especially in the East, religious traditionalism still maintains inviolable vocabularies of movement, in some cases so far removed from nature and spontaneous creativeness that dancers must begin training as young children when their bodies are capable of being molded along lines of abnormal movement.

In the Western world, the Renaissance, which has been greatly overvalued for its service to art, applied its passion for standardization to the courtly dance, and paved the way for the 'setting up in the seventeenth century of an academy in France under charter from the king to make laws for the ballet from which it has never completely separated itself. To be sure, there have arisen reformers from time to time who have preached the rebellious doctrine of a return to nature, and through the generations there have been changes of many kinds in the body of the laws, but an academic ballet still exists which works from a premise quite apart from creative movement.

Even in the nominally free tradition of the dance which has grown out of the revolt of Isadora Duncan there are now to be seen many manifestations of the same tendency to establish systems and ready-made vocabularies. Methods of movement which an individual dancer may have discovered to be expressive and logical for his own body with its particular conformations and for his own temperament and mental attitude, are frequently transformed into standard technics and superimposed upon pupils with whose temperaments and bodily conformations they have nothing in common.

All such crystallizations, historical and personal, together with selective aesthetic approaches and those deeper racial and geographical influences which tend to shape the dancer's practices, go to make up that aspect of dance which is known as style. A consideration of its broader values, both positive and negative, can perhaps be calculated to illuminate certain phases of the subject which are otherwise likely to be obscure.

Chapter Three

THE BASIS OF STYLE

❧❧❧❧❧

THE object in considering style is a purely practical one, namely, that works of art couched in unfamiliar idioms may become intelligible. The idea of translating from language to language for the sake of intelligibility is a common one, but it is not often recognized to what a large extent the same process must be employed with the languages of music, painting, architecture, dance. Time, place, race, religion, social customs, all make so deep an impression on the arts that it is possible to say that every group of people makes its art in a different language, or at least a different patois, and that none of them is totally familiar to any other group.

This point has not been stressed nearly as strongly as it deserves to be, with the result that where our art education is concerned we have been pretty thoroughly taken in by it, without any apparent realization of the process involved. Our attention has been directed almost exclusively to the translation of works from other times and other parts of the world, to the marked detriment of the artists who speak to us in our own tongue and of our own time. We have been so busy learning other people's languages, without even being aware that we were doing so, that we have remained virtually illiterate in our own. This is possibly only a by-product of our general educational tradition, for to adjust to an alien art expression demands a certain definite intellectual process, and this is no doubt more "educational" than merely to respond without any major adjustment to a work that speaks directly to our emotional understanding and does not necessitate such formal intellectual preparation.

Nevertheless, though contemporary native art, the expression of our own mind, is sorely neglected in favor of the old and the alien, the world teems with great works stemming from all peoples and all periods which only the most abysmal provincialism would advocate ignoring. Moments of illumination, of insight into human living, captured by artists in environments remote from our own, more than repay the effort that is required of us to penetrate through the purely local surfaces with which they have of necessity clothed their visions, to the universal core within. Sometimes the effort is beyond our capabilities, as in the case of much of the art of the East, and we are unable to get past the exoticism of the surface. At other times the adjustment is simple and after a bit of experience becomes practically automatic, just as one who learns to speak a foreign language and speaks it habitually over a long period acquires the ability to think directly in its terms without having to formulate his thought first in his own language. As an example of a similar art experience, we have grown so familiar with the music of the nineteenth century Germans that we have come to take it as our own language and are inclined to resent it when any other musical language is spoken even by our own composers.

It should never be forgotten, however, that an adjustment is necessary for all art created outside one's particular environment. The impulses of art, its motivations and its necessities, are universal, but the forms in which it is materialized are inevitably localized. Our guides to art appreciation do not always make this clear, and as a consequence leave us with a perhaps encyclopedic analysis of particular masterpieces but no hint of a general principle to work upon. Under no conditions can we expect to receive from a work of art out of another culture or another period a reaction identical with that which it produced in its own group, for the background out of which it sprang is too far removed from our experience. The more fully we can recreate this background synthetically at the back of our minds, the greater will be the reaction we enjoy, and the keener will be our appreciation of the essential truth which the artist has attempted to voice.

The danger of the entire process of adjustment, however, lies in the fact that studying alien art methods and remote backgrounds can become such an absorbing intellectual pursuit that it completely obliterates the function of works of art as such. Scholars are frequently to be found who know the most intimate details about whole periods of art and yet give no evidence of having ever really touched the aesthetic substance of any of it. This kind of scholarship is generally the resort of those whose natural response mechanism is not too vigorous, yet who are nevertheless attracted to art and eager to have closer contact with it. It is largely the result of developing the wrong instrument through unawareness of the right one. In any choice between the two instruments—intellectual knowledge and motor responsiveness—the latter is by far the more rewarding. The incidental facts and theories surrounding the arts will come of themselves bit by bit through continued association, though it is undeniably true that against a background of strong motor responsiveness, a little outside preparation can be stimulating and useful.

The basis of style goes back to the elementary fact that art is a form of compensation. As was pointed out earlier, the artist finds himself equipped with urgent potentialities which he cannot fulfill in his actual life environment, and creates a hypothetical environment in which these potentialities can be fulfilled. In the creation of this hypothetical environment he necessarily employs materials which are familiar to him. On these facts the structure of style is built: that every environment presents different limitations to be overcome, and offers different materials, including different patterns of behavior, as the agencies for overcoming them.

To take perhaps the most striking example, there is the contrast between those categories of art which belong to the south countries and those which belong to the north. Where nature is kind, food plentiful, shelter and clothing easily obtained, art is characterized by acquiescence. The artist does not struggle against nature, but seeks only to intensify the beneficence which he finds about him, to live ever more richly and fully. His music is melodious and voluptuous; his architecture is low and balanced, conforming to the line of the landscape and emphasizing it. In the northern countries all this is changed. Nature is not a willing ally but must be fought and tamed. Food is not easy to get, and must be stored for the future; shelter and clothing make large demands where bitter winds blow and half the year is burdened with snow and ice. Here art is characterized by a far greater intensification of the harmonious vision, for in it lies not pleasure alone but survival. In such art there are to be found purpose, determination, even defiance. The music stirs in emotional depths seeking to resolve doubts and unrests; the architecture rises at right angles to the line of the landscape, opposing it, and pointing upward into space with a gesture of freedom from the bondage of the earth.

A perfectly contented people might be expected to produce no art at all, since everything within their range of vision would already have been found to exist in life experience. In proportion as the vision of potential fulfillment exceeds the degree of present satisfaction, art takes on depth and substance and tends to transcend mere graciousness of surface. In the increasing complexity of contemporary Western civilization there is obviously a great incentive to creative art, in spite of the common opinion to the contrary. To an unprecedented extent man's vision of the possibilities of a fuller life and accomplishment has outrun his ability to realize in practical terms what he sees himself capable of, both individually and collectively, and the surplus must expend itself. That the art resulting from this expenditure is not more widely recognized as a great and characteristic expression is owing perhaps to the difference in its forms, its materials, its texture, from those of quieter, narrower and less idealistic times upon which we have been nurtured culturally.

In all times and in all places art has used the forms, materials, textures, with which it was familiar. To a great extent, these have been determined by geographical considerations, the rock, the soil, the weather, the type of raw stuff naturally available, and the social and economic systems that these have bred. Not only do such sources supply the actual stone for the architect and the sculptor, and the pigment for the painter, but they are responsible as well for the objects and the conditions of living which the artist pictures.

On the other hand, the nature of man himself unconsciously shapes his arts in his own image, for the determination of characteristic forms comes largely from within. By a kind of inversion of the process of "inner mimicry," we project ourselves into the forms of things we make just as we read our own impulses into the things we see. It is quite usual for the writer of dialogue to put his own phrases and habits of speech unconsciously into the mouths of his characters. Illustrators commonly put their own physical characteristics and postural habits upon the figures they draw. In a larger sense, it has been demonstrated that there is a marked unity of form between the physical qualities of the various racial types and their respective architectures. Irving K. Pond, following an earlier architect, Espérandieu, has dealt briefly but delightfully with the "ethnology of architectural forms" along these lines in *The Meaning of Architecture.*

Racial qualities of voice result in racial types of music, and even the instruments that are developed will tend to be those of similar timbres. Language itself grows similarly out of group thought and physical equipment. Certainly those peoples of the East whose legs are particularly supple and who sit on the floor instead of on chairs will evolve out of this single physical characteristic different forms of furniture, clothing, and social practice from those common to the Western world where legs are relatively stiff. There are infinite variations to be played on the theme, some of them built on readily apparent evidence, others so deeply rooted in unrationalized experience as to be virtually impossible of scientific verification. Art becomes thus clearly the product of the interplay between man and his environment, a fact that goes deeply to the roots of the whole subject.

Against the background of these fundamental distinctions, shaped and directed in the remotest periods of time, history marches through group cultures. Wars, the subjection of tribe by tribe, and nation by nation; empire; religious movements, philosophies, the establishment of ecclesiasticism; famines, plagues, pestilences; migrations, discoveries, inventions; revolutions, ideals of liberty, emancipations; industrialism, machinery, power—a tremendous succession of changing values, of sharpening cleavages, create new potentialities for man and along with them new limitations to their fulfillment. Manifestly the sympathetic response to any period's art lies far less in familiarity with how certain painters applied their color and certain musicians their harmony and counterpoint than with a grasp of the forces that controlled this eternal margin between the will of the time and its fruition.

Historical Periods

THE approach to the specific consideration of style in the dance differs rather widely from the approach in other arts, for the simple reason that the dance has no living past. It is possible to make firsthand contacts with works of art in virtually all other mediums at almost every stage of their historical development, but the dance of other periods is lost for lack of adequate recording. It is possible to make presumptive restorations from occasional fairly explanatory records, and there are traces of antiquity handed down, though with colossal changes, through folk practices, but generally speaking, there is no dance work that can be seen in its authentic state after it has once ceased to be performed regularly and passes into history.

For example, the oldest work now in the ballet repertory is Dauberval's "La Fille Mal Gardée," first produced in 1786 and still given from time to time chiefly by the Soviet State Ballets. That it is little more than a wraith of its original self, handed down from generation to generation by tradition, is safe to assume, and a solitary wraith at that, for none of its contemporaries remains to keep it company. From such a source as this there is obviously little to be learned of eighteenth century style, save by deduction.

Far younger works have been forgotten completely after brilliant successes in their own day. Of the great 1830-40 period, when romanticism captured the ballet, there remains not a single authentic work. "Giselle" has persisted continuously through the years, but it would be a dangerous business to guess how much of its original choreography survives. Popular ballets of the Petipa era are now chiefly disembodied reputations. Even so great a work as his "La Belle au Bois Dormant," first produced in 1890, had to be pieced together for revival in 1921 from notes and memories of dancers who had been associated with it in its previous incarnations, and then copiously filled in from other and more frankly imaginative sources. More recent works than this, however, have disappeared beyond hope of authentic revival. When Fokine was asked, shortly before the revival in 1935 of his "Thamar," originally created in 1912, if this was to be an accurate reproduction, he replied that he did not see how it could possibly be since even he himself did not remember it.

Of earlier days, nothing is to be looked for. Except for a bare handful of manuscripts in various methods of notation and not too readily decipherable, the entire court period, the time of Camargo and Sallé, the great reforms of Noverre, the works of Viganò, live only in historical reports about them and a few relevant technical data. On such external evidence as this, coupled with knowledge of the life of the times, must stylistic background be built.

No such condition exists in any other art, except perhaps that of the actor, which is really a subdivision of that of the dancer. In music, for example, scores are available from the early contrapuntalists, the troubadours, the madrigalists, and even before. There are the beginnings of opera, and ironically enough, the music for many of the early ballets. There are riches of all sorts from the seventeenth and eighteenth centuries, as well as the nineteenth and twentieth.

Perhaps something of the situation of the dance can be seen if a similar set of circumstances is imagined in music. Suppose in order to play a Tchaikovsky symphony, it were necessary to hunt up old musicians who had originally performed the work and piece together a score from their memories of what they had played! Or worse still, suppose that a Beethoven symphony had to be approximated from written accounts of its first performance supplemented by whatever knowledge could be gleaned from outside sources of the prevailing musical practices of the day and to what extent Beethoven conformed to them. The result would be at best an interesting thesis, but certainly not a symphonic score in any sense, and much less a particular score by Beethoven.

Revivals of old dance compositions are just as difficult as this and as unsatisfactory. Indeed, even the restoration of the general style of a period is altogether a matter of pastiche, and contains at least as much of the individual style and times of the artist making the restoration as it does of the period that is being restored.

The Greek dance provides an excellent illustration. There is nobody now living who has any definite knowledge of how the Greeks of the classic era danced, nor has any such knowledge existed in the world for many centuries. Nevertheless, for the past four hundred years at least there have been "revivals" of Greek dance. In the sixteenth century, under the influence of the Renaissance, musicians and poets were generally bent upon reestablishing the unities of the Greek choric drama. Ronsard, Baïf, and the group known as the Pléiade were active in Paris, and a few years later, Peri, Caccini, and the group known as the Camerata were even more active in Florence. Naturally, the dance was not unaffected. Fabritio Caroso records efforts to compose dances for the ballrooms of Italy in spondees and dactyls to ally dance thus with poetry in what was meant to be the manner of the ancient Greeks. In the court of Henry III of France, the "Ballet Comique de la Reine" told a story of Circe in a fashion which its creator, Beaujoyeux, and his contemporaries considered to be a well-realized restoration of the Greek choric drama, though its characters wore the còurt costumes of the time and the whole procedure differed from the customary court ballet of the day only in a somewhat greater unity of plot.

A century and a half later Greek gods and heroes peopled the ballet still clad in sumptuous elaborations of the contemporary court costume. In 1733 Marie Sallé created a scandal when she danced the role of Galatea without these trappings but in "a simple dress of muslin" which seemed to her to be more appropriate. A generation later Noverre was still somewhat radical when in his ballet, "La Toilette de Vénus," he left the conventional wide-skirted coat off his fauns, replaced the customary red-heeled shoe with a laced one suggesting the bark of a tree, and substituted for the customary white of gloves and stockings, a color to represent the flesh tint of "these forest inhabitants." A simple drapery of tiger skin covered part of the body, and the rest was allowed to give the appearance of nudity, but in order not to cause too violent a contrast with the costumes of the nymphs, a garland of flowers was thrown over the tiger skins.

In the days of Louis XVI and on into the next century, a new classical wave spread, stimulated by Winckelmann's researches into Greek art, and for the first time the ballet interested itself in a slightly more archeological style of dress for its continuing succession of Greek gods.

During none of these years had any thought whatever been given to the choreographic style that might have belonged to the ancients; instead there prevailed without question the fundamental vocabulary of movements established in the court ballet, crystallized in the academy of Lully, and revised and extended from within by the logical developments of time. Whether it even occurred to anybody that perhaps there was such a thing as a different idiom of movement seems altogether doubtful.

Indeed, at the end of the nineteenth century the idea seems to have been definitely established that there was not. Then in a dissertation on the antique Greek dance, Maurice Emmanuel examined sculpture and ceramic paintings and concluded that the Greek dance was much the same in vocabulary as the nineteenth century ballet. The bare feet depicted on dancing figures were often merely the result of an artist's convention, he contended, and he found reason to believe that the Greeks even danced on the points of their toes, though nobody else had ever done so, to be sure, until the Taglioni period. Significantly enough, Cecil Sharp, the eminent English folklorist, examining the same material a few years later, found it to contain many similarities to the contemporary folk dance of European peoples.

At the turn of our own century, Isadora Duncan, deeply impressed with Greek art but well aware that she was not in any sense reviving the antique dance, adopted the classic tunic as her costume, threw off corset, shoes and other time-honored impedimenta, including the technic of the ballet itself, and unwittingly started another Greek dance revival. In the Russian Ballet, Michel Fokine, a supreme stylist, created against a background of ballet training, though not in the traditional ballet manner, a number of Greek works, going for his source material to sculpture and ceramics, and achieving, at least in his "Daphnis and Chloe," a touch of the archaic manner of the ceramists. Nijinsky in his "L'Après-midi d'un Faune" employed a more exaggerated archaism of pose, working almost exclusively in the two-dimensional quality of a frieze. Virtually everywhere today there exists a type of simple, free and natural dance that calls itself Greek or "revived" Greek, though manifestly the "revival" is built on external information and intuition together with the example of Isadora Duncan, rather than on any actual knowledge of the antique dance. In Greece itself, Eva Sikelianos and Vassos Kanellos have separately re-created what their deep study of the subject has made each of them believe to be the essential spirit of the antique dance.

In the face of all these conflicting presentations, what is Greek classic dance style? Apparently it is whatever you think it is. In each of these instances, it is quite clear that the artist has looked at ancient Greece and given his individual interpretation of it, against the background of whatever his particular period has known about it archeologically and felt about it emotionally. It becomes necessary, then, to identify the period in which the style is evolved equally with that period at which it aims. Thus, if we would make ourselves clear, we must obviously refer to Renaissance Greek, or Louis Seize Greek, or Isadora Duncan Greek, or Russian Ballet Greek, for there is manifestly no such thing as objective Greek dance.

The situation is substantially the same when the dancer attempts to reproduce the style of any other period, though of course the Greek far outdistances all competitors in the race for popular approximation. It is not, however, a very calamitous situation. If there were dance works extant from other times, it would be vitally necessary to know how to present them, but in view of the fact that there are no such works pressing for performance, the occasion does not arise. Certainly there is as little reason for any dancer to set out to create an authentic dance in a remote style as there would be for a musician to compose an authentic fifteenth century madrigal or a writer to adopt the English of Chaucer. The creative artist may allow influences from the past to enrich his style, or he may deliberately quote from it, if to do so has point, or he may employ his special knowledge or intuition to create an impression of it, but he maintains his own approach and speaks inevitably to his own time. For the actor or the musician who is not an originator but a performer of an existing repertory extending back through the centuries, the case is somewhat different. It is imperative for him to have a knowledge of period and a sense of styles. Even here, however, the present colors his performance; he is interpreting and in a sense commenting upon another epoch, pointing out its characteristic flavors to his contemporaries. He lives in two worlds, as it were.

In the dance no such problem exists, for though many dancers perform what others compose for them, there is no repertory from the past to be concerned with. The nearest thing to such a problem is the approach to the traditional ballet, which in spite of a necessarily contemporary repertory retains certain fundamental principles established three hundred years ago and employs many traces of the past in its actual vocabulary of movement. It would be totally inaccurate, however, to consider the ballet style in itself as a period style, for it represents at bottom a particular approach to the dance which has nothing to do with time. The mere handful of specific works that have been handed down from earlier periods in word-of-mouth form are too few to constitute a problem. Illiteracy has taken care of that situation with devastating thoroughness.

The matter of period, then, presents little or no trouble to the spectator who has the average man's background of general history and social change, for the dance as we know it has no life outside the present. The limits of this present lie between the memory of the oldest dancer now active and the vision of the most forward-looking. It is within this range, then, that a practical consideration of style must function, rather than within some more orthodox range patterned after the necessities of the other arts.

Ethnic Influences

WITHIN the present there is only one category that presents serious obstacles, and these so serious, indeed, that they are in many cases insurmountable. This is the ethnic category. It is to all intents and purposes impossible for a Westerner to grasp the subtleties and symbolism of the dance arts of the East, intricately interwoven as they are with religion and social custom. For their decorative values, their unusual color, and their stimulation of interest through the sheer difference in their movement vocabularies they are frequently admired and applauded, but rarely, it is safe to say, for the proper reasons from the dancer's point of view.

In a certain degree this is also true of that ancient and highly involved composite that we call loosely the Spanish dance. Deeply rooted in the life and spirit of the people, it retains still the qualities of a folk expression even when it is taught with classic precision to the daughters of the élite or transplanted bodily to the stage. With the strong flavor of the East in its mobility of body, the constantly centripetal emphasis of its curving lines, its awareness of the earth beneath it, its passion and petulance, its bursts of song, the counterpoint of its castanets, snapping fingers and heel rhythms, its inviolable and inexplicable traditions make of it a magnificent, complex and utterly unique manifestation. La Argentina, by her genius for the theater and her impeccable taste, translated it into a universality which it generally does not have. Lacking such unique illumination, however, it is best approached as the exciting expression of a richly passionate people, and admired simply for what it seems to be. To grasp its many subtleties and traditionalisms can easily become a career in itself.

Possibly because in exotic types of dance it is only the surface that is seen and this seems striking and delightful, a quantity of pseudo-ethnic dancing has come into existence, reproducing sometimes most painstakingly all the superficial detail of the original, apparently with the firm belief on the dancer's part that he has penetrated to the heart of the matter. For the experienced spectator, even though he is without technical knowledge, the difference is readily recognizable, sensed rather than rationally understood. It is far easier to speak a foreign language without a trace of accent than it is to dance in a foreign idiom with complete purity of style. Indeed, if the former is difficult, the latter is practically impossible, for movement rises in the unintellectualized realm of experience and is likely to betray the pretender in spite of his most assiduous mental effort.

Ethnic influences, however, employed frankly as such, form a useful part of the dancer's resources, especially in the field of the ballet. It was part of Fokine's great reform in this medium that when its plots dealt with other races its movements should also conform to racial styles. Previously it had been the practice to make no differentiation whatever, but to present the peoples of all times and places in the conventional vocabulary of the academic ballet, and even to costume them in the standardized ballet costume of tights, fluffy tulle skirts, pink slippers, etc. The ladies dressed their hair in the latest fashion and wore any jewels they were lucky enough to possess, without regard for the racial or financial status of the characters they chanced to be portraying. The only nod in the direction of style consisted of a bit of characteristic decoration, such as a narrow border of Greek or Egyptian design on the edge of the skirt, an apron if the character happened to be a peasant maid, or a few beads and a quill in the hair for an Indian. Fokine put a definite end to all such practices. For him Greeks, Hindus, Egyptians, Persians, as well as the many native tribes of his own Russia, moved in a manner dictated by the most reliable research.

To say that such movement is authentic would be to misstate the case entirely, for authentic movement would simply get in the way of the artist's creative purpose in much the same way that the everyday naturalistic gesture would. The ballet itself is a convention of the Western theater, and though its choreographic action must be adapted to give the color of other styles it must remain always within the bounds of its own. Such a method is familiar in the musician's world. Remote ethnic melodic practices, rhythms and timbres are approximated by the conventional instruments of the Western orchestra and in the conventional Western musical forms. It is unheard of for any Western musician to compose authentic Eastern music, and the "Scheherazades" and the "Madame Butterflies" are frankly intended to be evocative rather than ethnically accurate.

Outside the ballet, there is the striking example of Ruth St. Denis and her many Oriental dances. The great majority of them were created before she had ever put foot in the Orient and were not meant to be museum pieces but a Western vision into an Eastern art. Their music, like Fokine's, was part of the approximation and made no pretense to authenticity.

Ethnic style, then, like period style, demands qualifications. Just as we must speak of Renaissance Greek and Louis Seize Greek, so we must speak of Fokine Chinese and St. Denis Hindu. The style of the artist who makes the adaptation is at least as important as that of the original dance being reproduced. The whole approach to both ethnic and period styles in the contemporary dance, therefore, resolves itself into a deliberate process of evocation by synthetic means. It consists in extracting a certain essence from authenticity and employing it to give flavor to the whole, with no notion of archeological or ethnological accuracy. It is dictated, in the same degree that considerations of form are dictated, by the dual necessity of the artist to say what he has to say and to say it with due regard for the capacity of response that he can count on from his audience.

Unfortunately, out of such a perfectly sound aesthetic practice abuses have grown, and countless stylistic clichés have come into existence and been accepted in certain quarters as standard. Instead of going to original sources, it has been easier to go to some artist's successful adaptations and take them as a routine vocabulary. It does not matter at all that the same artist has probably employed a totally different approach and even different materials in other dances deriving from the same ethnic or period background. Thus we see a kind of standard Egyptian dance which presupposes that the ancients were exclusively two-dimensional creatures and that their representation in the early paintings was realistic portraiture. In this same category of art, Chinese dancers always shuffle about either with hands in sleeves or with index fingers pointing upward; "Orientals" are a half-clad composite of India and the state-fair midway, and indulge almost entirely in undulations of the hips accompanied by ripples of the arms. There are similar stereotypes to be found under the labels of Greek, Japanese, Russian, American Indian, Negro, Spanish, Dutch, and even "peasant." These are perhaps best classified as dancing school styles, but, unhappily, so to classify them does not remove them from the scene where they do a great deal of damage in the shaping of popular taste.

If there are distinctive differences of style to be found between groups of people who are of various races, cultures and backgrounds, there are also countless deviations from the particular norm within each group. Indeed, it is necessary to consider style as without any very clearly determinable boundaries, and certainly not as a static and specific thing that can be neatly pigeonholed. It varies markedly from individual to individual, and in the arts this is an element of some importance. The outstanding artist is invariably endowed with a highly personal style, inescapably related, it is true, to the style of the group of which he is a member and an interpreter, but departing from the norm of the group in indefinable ways. To describe or account for the particularities of personal style is as impossible as to describe or account for the particularities of physiognomy or complexion. In its less attractive phases it manifests itself as mannerisms and eccentricities, but when it belongs to a poised and richly endowed artist, it transcends surface trivialities and becomes a kind of luminous epitome of individuality.

Such qualities are easily recognized even in mediums in which the vocabulary and methods of procedure are codified and fixed by tradition. In the realm of the academic ballet, for example, an intangible combination of forces sets Alicia Markova apart, as it set Anna Pavlova apart, though the vocabulary of movement is the same academic vocabulary that is used by hundreds of other dancers. If we go farther afield into the alien art of the Spanish dance, the great exponents of our day, La Argentina, Argentinita, and Escudero furnish even more notable examples, as different from each other as possible, yet all elevated far above the rank and file of Spanish dancers by subtleties of carriage, of insight into the use of materials, of intuitive flavor.

The freer type of dance which follows in the footsteps of Isadora Duncan has recognized the existence of individuality to such an extent that it has built its approach largely on this ground. Mere freedom from established routine, however, does not automatically produce greatness of personal style, and it is still some inexplicable balance of factors that results in a Mary Wigman or a Martha Graham.

Ironically enough, we find that in this field of dance that is based on personal vision and personal style and is meaningless without them, the very strength of the theory is in danger of becoming its weakness. The emergence of striking personalities with highly individual manners of moving has led to little coteries of disciples at the feet of each, modeling their movements, their styles, their approach to costuming, composition, content, as closely as possible upon those of their leaders, utterly unmindful of the fact that they are denying the very theory of the type of dance they have embraced. Thus personal style is seen to lead to crystallizations just as ethnic and period styles do, retaining in each case only the surface aspects of a fresh and creative art adventure, erecting out of them a standardized vocabulary and a traditional approach and setting up new classicisms beside the old.

Classicism and Romanticism

TREMENDOUS confusions exist with regard to the relationships between classicism, romanticism and modernism in the dance. No sooner do we get it all straightened out on what seems to be a perfectly satisfactory basis that the ballet is altogether classic, the dance of Isadora Duncan and the "interpretative" school romantic, and that of Wigman, Graham and Humphrey modern, than we begin to hear troublesome rumors. Some one will talk, for example, of the romantic ballet of Taglioni, and as if that were not enough in itself, will add bewilderingly that though this was romantic, it is really what we mean today by classic. Some one else will make disturbing references to Fokine both as a master of the ballet and as a romantic revolutionist, or Isadora will be declared to be a modern, or Kurt Jooss will be said to make ballets out of modern dance.

To resolve these difficulties in a categorical manner is not to bring any fundamental enlightenment to the subject as a whole. Indeed, before it is possible to discuss any of these artists or their characteristic styles, there must be some clarification of the main issue, for we are inclined to be rather cloudy about these three selective aesthetic approaches in themselves quite apart from the dance.

For example, when a work of art is said to be classical, it may prove to be any one of six things: it may have to do with ancient Greece or Rome; it may be a work from another period that has managed to survive, usually in the schoolroom; it may be composed according to specific and stereotyped rules of form; it may employ a standard, codified vocabulary; it may be couched in a style that is cool, unemotional and neatly balanced in design; or it may be simply something outside the range of what is immediately and cheaply popular. Thus we find the academic ballet and the dance of Isadora Duncan, the symphonies of Haydn and those of Tchaikovsky, the *Iliad* and *Uncle Tom's Cabin,* all subjected to the same epithet!

Romanticism is likely to suggest to us lovers meeting clandestinely by moonlight or wasting away with phthisis, for we have inherited from our fathers that flavor of the tag-end of the last century. If we were asked to define modernism, we should find it virtually impossible to do so without resort to such words as angularity, cacophony, intellectualism, and it would be an effort to keep away from neurosis, decadence and primitivism.

All three of these approaches, however, are historic influences closely related to the life of the times in which they have developed, and in their periodic alternations and recurrences they have in every case arisen out of the essential drives of a particular environmental situation. Only a recourse to history, therefore, can clarify their fundamental natures by revealing the living impetus behind them, and save them from being treated as nothing but opposing "schools."

Perhaps the definitive character of classicism consists in its guidance by objective criteria and its faith in the cumulative wisdom of traditional procedure.

In the direct line of the arts of the Western world, it has its beginning in the Hellenistic period, with Alexander the Great as its father and Aristotle certainly in no lesser capacity than that of godfather. Before this time, it is true, great works of the past were reverenced; Homer and the glowing figures of the fifth century had long been part of a prized and consciously permanent background. Even before the rise of Greek culture there had been libraries of some magnificence in Egypt and Babylonia. When Alexander swept across the scene, however, the attitude toward the past's accumulation of artistic and intellectual treasures was vastly changed, and with it the future of Western culture. With a passion for Hellenizing that far exceeded mere avariciousness or political ambition, he embraced the whole barbarian world in the name of the Greek way of life. The culture of Greece had been spreading outside its own borders slowly and genuinely for many years by reason of its inherent persuasiveness; now the process was intensified manyfold, and the authority of Greek pre-eminence was established by official action. Local rulers and subrulers hastened to assume and advocate the utmost of Greekishness irrespective of conviction, and everything Hellenic became the fashion.

Obviously, this could be nothing but a forced culture over a large area of the civilized world. The native creativeness of the conquered peoples was stifled under this onrush of official superiority. Libraries were established, the great works of Greek writers were collected, studied, and diligently copied. That there was an enormous increase in specific cultural activity cannot be questioned, but whether its tendencies toward pedanticism and self-consciousness represented any advance in ultimate values over the natural and living manifestations that it displaced and destroyed is another matter.

In Alexandria in the third century B.C. we find the organized study of the foremost writers, orators, and philosophers of the past under way, critical editions of Homer being issued, and, what interests us most at the moment, lists drawn up of those writers who were officially decreed by the scholars to be best. It was still a long time before such selected works were actually called classics, but that is what they were in fact. The term itself did not arise until five centuries later in the Roman period, when the grammarian, Aulus Gellius, made a parallel between various grades of writers and the classes of Roman society. His comparison took as its model the social division set up in the ancient constitution attributed to Servius Tullius, in which all men were divided into six classes on a basis of property, the highest being the classici, and the lowest or propertyless, the proletarii. To this scheme Gellius made the writer conform, the highest type being denominated a scriptor classicus and the lowest a scriptor proletarius. Thus the classics were specifically named and defined, and endowed with a kind of snobbism that has extended far beyond the day of Gellius.

So great was the effect of Alexander's conquest upon a posterity more remote than he could even have envisioned in his day, that we still find the barbarian world being supplied with its lists of officially correct art out of the past and its correlative rules of officially acceptable procedure for the creation of art in the present. The artist who makes bold to violate these laws pronounces himself, today as in ages past, a barbarian and an aesthetically propertyless, ungrounded proletarian. It is interesting to note that the concern in the first place is exclusively with literature, and that it is literary men who make up the approved lists. Apparently none of the other arts seemed to them important enough to bother with.

At any rate, if the select works of literature and the canonized methods of guaranteeing this same selectness for the future were maintained in all their purity, history was conforming to no such carefully regulated pattern. Dynasty followed dynasty, power succeeded power, until in the early years of the Middle Ages life is seen to be rather remote from Hellenism, for all the careful nurture of the classics. The very language of the classics of the Alexandrians has by now become unintelligible to all save a handful of scholars, and even the literary Latin of more recent centuries is known only to the clergy and the courtiers.

The common speech does not derive from the highly inflected literary language but is a purely colloquial tongue. Being a part of the daily life of the ordinary man, free, colorful, utilitarian, it evolves its rules out of the necessities of communication, and not from academic code and culture. Such a system makes, of course, for diversity rather than standardization, each group slowly developing its own variations to fill its own requirements. In those days, that part of the world that had constituted the old Roman Empire was known as Romania, and its various dialects, developed from the popular spoken Latin that had been the basic tongue, came, naturally enough, to be referred to as Romanic or Romance languages. The tales sung or written in these languages were dubbed, accordingly, romances.

They were ebullient tales, indeed, unrestrained by convention, dealing with the adventures of common men, rogues, and fighters, with the exploits of kings and heroes out of classic myth and tradition, with intrigues of lovers and their mistresses, with magic, religion and superstition. They were, in short, the result of the necessity of the people to produce an art based on their own background and containing compensations growing out of their common life. When the works of the scriptores classici become increasingly remote and unrewarding, then scriptores proletarii must arise to supply the demands for that satisfaction that art alone can give.

The romancers, then, are closer to life and to spontaneous creation than their classic superiors, in spite of the fact that they do not bother with realism, that they indulge in the freest kind of fantasy, that they disregard probability and logic, and that they frequently allow their characters to lapse into the most wooden of types. In romanticism we see a return to feeling as a guide rather than form and precedent. As some one has said of it, if it ignored the classic unities of time, place and action, it supplied a new unity of compelling interest. This it achieved not by taking pains, but by sheer inward vitality. It is the democratic as opposed to the aristocratic art, a democracy of the imagination bordering at times on anarchism.

Between these two doctrines of classicism and romanticism, the history of the arts, controlled to be sure by the history of the life about them, swings back and forth, if not always in world cycles, at least in small waves within virtually every period. It is apparently nature's habit to effect progress in this manner of alternation, for even plant growth is seen to take place, not in a straight line, but first on one side and then on the other. The unfortunate aspect of the pendulum method, however, as it applies to culture, is that at each extreme a residue is thrown off that exhibits a deplorable hardihood, and manages to set up a tenacious existence in an orbit of its own, stolidly unaffected by the life around it. Thus in the twentieth century we are still faced with accumulations of Renaissance academism which clutter our educational systems and hang on the neck of our art criticism with the stubbornness of the Old Man of the Sea.

With the great dawn of the Renaissance there comes a mighty swing back to classicism. This is a strictly aristocratic movement patterned on inaccurate but idealistic visions of the classicism of ancient Greece and Rome. An awkward, wealthy, blousy upper class, weary of the age-old domination of medieval mysticism, has caught sight of an orderliness of mind and a personal elegance that once were the prerogatives of its forebears, and it sets out to attain them for itself with a fervor that is, amusingly enough, very like the exuberance of romanticism.

As a matter of fact, the impulse of the early Renaissance, like that of its correlative movement in the North, the Reformation, was essentially romantic. Though it lacked the genuinely democratic basis of romanticism, being wholly a movement of the ruling classes, it partook in a degree of the same quality in that it was a breaking away from superimposed codes of thought and practice for the attainment of individual expression. The particular manifestation of classicism against which it rebelled was that of the medieval religious system which dominated all thinking and made every man no more than an insignificant cog on an ominous wheel of dubious function. This system, in its turn, had once been a truly romantic movement in the basic sense of the word, for primitive Christianity was a mass demand for spiritual democracy, a demand that grew upwards through the ranks of society beginning with the slaves. Only with the crystallizations of ecclesiasticism did it pass into sterility and formula.

The ultimate weakness of the revolt of the Renaissance nobles lay in the fact that it had no such solid groundings to support it as either the early Christian movement or medieval romanticism had had; it never succeeded in getting down to bedrock, but merely substituted one type of classicism for another with no loss of authoritarianism but only a transfer of authority. The more durable results of the Reformation, for all that it, too, lapsed into petty bickerings and the establishment of many little orthodoxies, are perhaps attributable to the greater depth of its romanticism, that is, its superior democratic impulsion.

But the Renaissance was a movement of that element of society that Servius Tullius had denominated classici, and its ideals for the liberation of the individual from medieval suppression stopped with the restoration of a cultural life conforming, logically enough, to Aulus Gellius's category of classicus. The new vision had no meaning whatever for the common man.

To insure no relapses into medieval crudeness, academies were set up in every walk of life, with codes and rules for virtually everything, under official authority of the ruling sovereign. A select list of Greek and Roman masters became the standard for all style, and imitations and restorations of ancient culture were as exact as current scholarship allowed, which in many instances was undoubtedly very inexact, indeed. As Cicero was the model for all contemporary prose, so the original academy which he had headed as the last of a long line of scholarly succession from Plato, was, in spirit at least, exhumed as a model for the standardization of all cultural activities. Apparently Erasmus was the only devoted advocate of a broadly revived Greek and Roman scholarship who dared to criticize the fashionable apings of the day, and when he raised his voice to declare that "we must adapt ourselves to the age we live in, an age that differs completely from Cicero's," he was shouted down with abuse. To be sure, much of the ancient reviving was so copiously adapted to the age, however unwittingly, that even Erasmus, if he could have viewed it with sufficient perspective, would not have found the imitation too exact, for all the slavishness of its intention.

There can be no doubt that the impulse of the early Renaissance to abandon the sprawling remnants of decadent medieval romanticism and return to orderliness and intelligibility of form was a healthy and a creative one, a swing toward the center of balance after the pendulum had touched one of its extremes. But it was soon to swing to the other extreme and achieve a lifeless standardization, the only value of which lay in its unavoidable tendency to produce still another swing toward the center.

The ebbing of the Renaissance was followed by a movement that was in its turn quite as great a rebirth. Already in the baroque period emotional feeling had begun to make itself felt as against the restraints of classicism, and in the rococo with all its futile and meaningless elaborations there is an indication at least that fantasy and caprice have refused to be held down any longer and have got out of hand. The full revolt against classicism, however, does not make itself felt until the momentous eighteenth century has got well under way, but its roots go back at least as far as the philosophers of the Reformation who saw the essential nature of the individual man to be of supreme importance. On this basis all the revolutions of the century—political, social and artistic—were fought and won. The model for action was now no longer what the Greeks had done or what the scholars made of their doings, but nature itself as each man was able to know it without benefit of authority.

The new romanticism of the eighteenth century at best, however, was certainly far from realistic, for it dealt, as its medieval forerunner had done, with adventure, high emotion, fantastic and even supernatural extravagances; but it was concerned fundamentally with the emotional experiences of men, exaggerated and distorted though they might become in the process. Eventually, the tangible past, as opposed to the Olympian world of the classicists, became a living field of interest, the Middle Ages themselves assumed a new value in retrospect, becoming at last almost as much a source of material as Greece and Rome had been for the classicists. Their tales were refurbished and retold.

The personal passions of love and hate, of heartbreak and revenge, replaced the heroic aloofness of the old routine.

The Romantic Revolution, as it has been called, did not reach its climax until the early years of the next century, and within a generation afterwards it had spent its force. The clearest statement of its credo in its final period is to be found in the young Victor Hugo's preface to his play, *Cromwell*. Nineteenth century romanticism is seen much more markedly than that of the century before to present two complementary faces. In the first place, it represents, as it did in its earlier medieval manifestation, as definitely a Christian viewpoint as classicism represented a pagan one. Christianity itself, however, had undergone many changes, owing largely to the rise of Protestantism, and romanticism accordingly had a different philosophic flavor. It is now concerned deeply with personal morality and virtue, with the duality of good and evil and the consequent conflict in man, with the superiority of the soul over the grossness of the flesh. It indulges in flights of fancy over disembodied spirits, and voices a persistent yearning for higher ethereal spheres. It is easy to see how this approach, sincere and convinced though it might be in its beginnings, would slip easily, in its decadence, into sentimentality and sanctimoniousness.

The other face of the movement is its regard for nature with a particular emphasis upon pictures of folk life and peasant custom. To our taste as we look back at it, it seems prettified and superficial, but against its own background it had a certain lustiness which offset the contemporary concern for the more attenuated and unearthly qualities of the spirit. Rousseau had seen the two aspects as one, the simple passions of men related inseparably to the environment of nature, but the vigor of the romantic-democratic eighteenth century revolution had begun to wane, and passed steadily into greater and greater artificiality, ending in an atmosphere of trivial and saccharine insincerities which completely denied the vitality and the power that underlie true romanticism.

From this cursory summary, though it is chiefly along lines of literary development since both classicism and romanticism are literary terms, it is possible to sketch in a background against which these two antithetical approaches begin to assume their respective identities. Romanticism in every case precedes classicism, for it deals with content and substance where classicism is concerned with form and surface. It is matter where classicism is manner. It is spontaneous and demands participation of its audience, where classicism is reflective and invites observation. It is in effect emotional where classicism is mental; it induces excitement instead of balanced admiration; it is energetic and exuberant where classicism is poised and orderly; it seeks to awaken sympathetic experience instead of that combination of aesthetic responses that is generally described as beauty. Romanticism delights in things discovered, classicism in things made. Classicism is inevitably the development of material that has been uncovered by romantic impulses, for these are the forces that delve into experience and unearth its truths. No art movement, accordingly, ever begins by being classical; classicism is a second stage, a selective and refining stage.

The true classicist necessarily has a keen sense of style; that is to say, he is alert to the limitations of his chosen method of procedure, and deliberately pits his skill against his self-selected obstacles. If he is able to do this and take pleasure in it, he may succeed in achieving a high degree of effectiveness, and his technical adeptness becomes rather like the brilliant playing of a game. If he chooses to employ well-established forms such as the sonnet or the sonata, or well-established vocabularies like that of the academic ballet, he invites an easier response because his audience is familiar with the rules of the game and better able to applaud him when he scores. This intellectual framework exactly suits the temperament of those artists who are innately reticent, however deep their passions, and who seek restraining forms in order that, as Theodore Watts-Dunton said with reference to the sonnet, "the too fervid spontaneity and reality of the poet's emotion may be in a certain degree veiled, and the poet can whisper, as from behind a mask, those deepest secrets of the heart which could otherwise only find expression in purely dramatic forms." It is not an exploratory or an adventurous approach, but in those rare instances in which the artist's formal skill is animated by his awareness of the style he is embarked upon and is illuminated by the glow of living feeling, it can result in exquisite moments of contemplative beauty. But the pitfalls of sterile academism are many and deep along its way.

The approach of the romanticist is along the path of nature and subjective experience. He works not by rule but by revelation, trusting to his sensitiveness to himself and to his fellows to guide him to the adequate communication of emotional adventure. His peril is "self-expression" carried to the borders of emotional debauchery and resulting in formlessness and incoherence.

Modernism

MODERNISM (or what we call modernism today, for it is an inclusive term) has arisen to save him from these perils, since its characteristic drive is toward functional form. In modernism, as in classicism and romanticism, we are faced with a movement that is in no sense arbitrary but has manifestly grown out of its environment. Indeed, it is inconceivable that it could have come about at any other period of history, for it is directly related to the development of the machine, of power, of technology.

Contrary to the common assumption, it has not merely taken over these developments by contagion and mechanized itself; to read no more than that into its origin is to miss one of the salient aspects of its nature. That it has profited by the efficiency and the essential economy of the machine by which it is able to accomplish large ends with small means, is undeniable, but there is a deeper relationship to be sought. It is in a sense a repetition of the process by which romanticism came to birth in the Middle Ages. Then the classic culture had become so remote from the common man that he had no art and was forced to make himself one. Now something of the same sort had happened; technology had destroyed the current concept of art, which had been built up for many generations on the ideal of representationalism. Verisimilitude, the be-all and the end-all of art for so long, had ceased to be the business of the artist at all; it was accomplished now with genuine efficiency by any number of recording devices. There was no longer any sense in the artist's attempting to evoke wonder by his camera-like eye or his phonograph-like ear; he was clearly outdistanced, another victim of technological unemployment!

This mechanical inferiority to the machine, however, served to reveal to him the possibilities in his own medium, and he awoke to see that what was valuable in art was its very incapacity to represent nature with this infallible accuracy. If he compared his paintings, for example, with their subjects, he could not fail to see that where the camera could only picture them as they were, he had actually pictured them as he saw them, which was not the same thing at all. Among the personal limitations that kept him from mechanical perfection were taste, selectivity, and subtle psychological quirks in his mentality that somehow projected themselves upon the canvas in spite of him. Here lay a virtually unused power of interpretation. He had touched, indeed, upon the principle of abstraction, the principle by which the essential qualities of an object or an experience or a concept could be abstracted from the mass of irrelevancies surrounding it and given more value than nature itself had given them. Here lay the complete answer to representationalism, the complete defiance of the machine in art.

His goal now, far from being the reproduction of the already familiar in the common daily round for no other end than the pleasure of recognition, became the production of the unfamiliar out of this same round, utilizing the pleasure of recognition only as the taking-off place for an expedition into untried emotional fields. Instead of dealing always with the objective surface of life, which has long enjoyed the title of "nature," it was now possible for him to deal with essences, to penetrate ever deeper into the subjective roots of experience.

The process of abstraction renounces all obligations toward fullness of detail, fidelity of proportion, and outward considerations of verisimilitude. The artist retains from the realism of his subject matter only those dominant elements that accord with his intention, and these he makes more vivid, more intense, larger than life, stripped clean and taut and naked. From the standpoint of literalism, this is nothing less than distortion, but since nothing could be farther from his mind than to produce a facsimile of anything, there is no real distortion involved. He is not mutilating outward reality; he is creating a new and independent object known as a work of art, an expression of his mind, in which he uses certain aspects of outward reality merely as a base of supplies.

These processes make the artist of necessity something of a technologist in his own sphere. The easy approach to composition which allowed early romanticists to relax and lean on nature is closed to him, and it is incumbent upon him to find active and vital forms in which to demonstrate his dynamic inventions. For this he must look not only to what he has to say, but also to the means, the materials, the medium, in which to say it. If he were trying to create an illusion of nature, instead of to produce a self-acknowledged work of art, he would minimize these matters, and do everything in his power to make the spectator believe that he was not in the presence of materials, means, medium, at all, but of nature itself. But he is making something called a painting, or a sculpture, or a dance, and in each case the materials with which he is working will have something to say about how he handles them. In his pursuit of functional forms, therefore, he must know first of all the nature of his materials, whether they happen to be sound, color, or movement, before he can shape them according to their inherent laws into being the outward body of his intent. They must collaborate on a virtually equal basis with his personal perspective on his subject matter in the determination of the shapes, the manner, the degrees, of his abstractions.

With the gaining of this point of view, he has found a new freedom. As a painter he no longer tries to make flat surfaces give the illusion of three dimensions, as a sculptor he quits forcing stone to pretend to be flesh, as an architect he abandons the practice of disguising steel structure as Gothic masonry, as a dancer he no longer hides behind the attitudinizing of a Greek god or a fairy prince. Movement, steel, stone and pigment are all seen to have unsurpassable qualities in their own characters without having always to be made to masquerade as something else, to represent objects instead of presenting concepts.

If the abandonment of representationalism has more importance for the romanticist—that is, for the artist who is concerned with expressing something—than it has for the classicist, whose art has no direct concern with life experience to begin with, nevertheless the modern accent on functional form presents the latter also with a new range of activity. It allows him to abandon traditional procedure and to let his materials lead him into new structural fields by their own natures. Compositions in pure color, line as line, mass as mass, sound as sound, are eminently practical with no expressional intent whatever. Of the dance, of course, this is only partially true, for the body cannot be separated from implied intent. Even here, however, experiments have been made in which the body is completely disguised within architectural constructions, though whether this still remains within the category of dance is open to question.

The modern classicist may or may not go as far as Stravinsky advocates, but he will at least recognize the essence of the neoclassic doctrine when he reads in the composer's autobiography that for him "music is, by its very nature, essentially powerless to *express* anything at all, whether a feeling, an attitude of mind, a psychological mood, a phenomenon of nature" but that "its indispensable and single requirement is construction." He may be undoctrinaire enough to dissent from this dictum in the belief that it is impossible thus to have pure construction suspended, as it were, in mid-air, and that there must always be something specific constructed. Nevertheless, he will have a marked sympathy for Stravinsky's further statement that "one could not better define the sensation produced by music than by saying it is identical with that evoked by contemplation of the interplay of architectural form." Again, it is doubtful that a few stray beams tastefully arranged in space without function could be called architectural forms, but the general meaning is clear.

As in every genuinely creative period, the germ of life is in the romantic section of the modern field. By having evolved a solid approach to form that is at one with the very basis of romanticism, modernism has effectually prevented the fulsomeness and rant that have frequently characterized romantic revivals, and has turned the seething energy of the romantic impulse into channels of restraint and intelligibility. The resultant approach has sometimes been called expressionism, and it would be difficult to devise a more fitting label.

Modernism is in every respect an unsatisfactory term to apply to so definite a manifestation, for it is in no sense descriptive. Certainly expressionism is not the first manifestation of modernism in history, but is only the form it has taken in our day. Indeed, modernism in the large sense is that tendency in any period which first senses and makes tangible the new directions of its time before they have become an accepted part of daily life. It is that trend which runs counter to the inertias of the day, whatever they may be, and is prophetic of the next level of artistic awareness. It is thus manifestly impossible to tie down; sometimes it is classical in tendency, sometimes romantic, and sometimes, as at present, it cuts squarely across both fields. Obviously, no matter what form it takes, it is inevitably strange and unpopular in the days of its ascent.

The ability to make independent judgments based on immediate personal response is essential to the enjoyment of modern art, for it relies on no teachings or academies, but deals with absolute values in a thoroughly direct and even pragmatical way.

If such a digression as this does not dissolve all the mysteries of Taglioni's romantic-classicism or Isadora's modern-romanticism or Jooss's classic-modernism, at least it prepares the ground for their discussion when in due course the occasion arrives.